KOEI-KAN KARATE-DO

Author (standing) with Master
Onishi Eizo,1990

KOEI-KAN KARATE-DO

PRACTICE AND PRECEPT

BRIAN FROST

FROG, LTD.
BERKELEY, CALIFORNIA

Published by Frog, Ltd.
Frog Ltd. books are distributed by North Atlantic Books
P.O. Box 12327
Berkeley, California 94712

Cover photo by Jeffrey Mason
Cover design by Andrea du Flon
Book design by Nancy Koerner
Distributed to the book trade by Publishers Group West

Library of Congress Cataloging-in-Publication Data

Frost, Brian, 1951–
       Koei-kan karate-do : practice and precept / Brian Frost.
             p.   cm.
       ISBN 1-883319-64-1
       1. Karate--History. 2. Karate--Philosophy. 3. Karate--Training.
       I. Title.
       GV1114.3.F76   1997
       796.815'3--dc21   97-15788
                                                                CIP

1   2   3   4   5   6   7   8   9   /   00   99   98

DEDICATION

There is no human being who more truly expresses the spirit of the art that has been labeled *Koei-Kan* than its founder, Onishi Eizo (Kancho *Sensei*). He is the sole creator of this art to which I have dedicated myself these many years. Words can never fully convey the nonrepayable debt *(Gimu)* that I owe to this Master. He is a great innovator, philosopher, historian, technician, pedagogue, and, more important, a great humanitarian. He comes from an exalted Samurai tradition, yet he is truly humble. His is not a false humility, but one that is born of both physical and academic excellence. Onishi Kancho *Sensei* has trained under, and been a leading pupil of, many Japanese, Okinawan and Chinese Masters of martial arts. He has developed and founded a second art, which he has termed *Kendo Gaku,** or "the study of the way of the fist." He feels that this new curriculum will be a contributing factor in the constructive future progression of humankind. The Master has taught and demonstrated throughout Asia, Europe, Latin America, and the United States. He is deserving of all the recognition and praise that he has so assiduously avoided. I am cognizant of the fact that this special man, whom I term *Meijin* (wizard in the martial arts and ways), is beyond my complete understanding. It is in this spirit that I pen this somewhat inadequate outline of *Koei-Kan Karate-Do*. I can only hope that the Master forgives my lack of knowledge and what he may perceive as any misrepresentation of his teachings and philosophy.

Kendo—The study of the way of the fist; it should not be confused with *Kendo* the way of the sword. In Japanese, *Ken,* while pronounced the same, is defined by two separate characters. One means fist. The other meaning sword.

Master Onishi Eizo, founder of the *Koei-Kan* System of *Karate-Do*

HONORABLE MENTION

I t would be a grave and unforgivable error to omit the immeasurable contributions that have been made to the introduction and promulgation of the *Koei-Kan Karate-Do* system outside of Japan by the one individual most responsible for said furtherance.

Edward Kaloudis (Kaloudis *Sensei*, to those of us who practice this laudable art) is without doubt the major pioneer of *Koei-Kan* in the United States, Europe, and Latin America.

Kaloudis *Sensei*, of Greek origin, began his martial arts training in judo. As a youth in the early 1950's, he became a cabinboy on a Greek freighter bound for Japan. The ship's captain was a practitioner of both judo and karate, as his ship often docked in Japan. It is through this circumstance that Kaloudis *Sensei* was introduced to Onishi Kancho *Sensei* and was subsequently accepted as his pupil. Eventually obtaining the grade of *Nidan* (second degree black belt), Kaloudis *Sensei* settled in the United States and began teaching *Koei-Kan* in New York City while a student at New York University in 1956. He later established his headquarters in New Jersey. He has taught and demonstrated throughout the world. He currently holds a *Hachidan*/eighth degree black belt, and serves as the United States Executive Director of *Koei-Kan Karate-Do* as well as International liaison.

Further recognition need be given to Mr. Gary Clements (a personal mentor of this author), who while serving in the United States Navy was stationed in Japan and studied under Onishi Kancho *Sensei*. He then returned to the United States to teach a select few in the Detroit metropolitan area.

Mention must also be made of Mr. Richard "Woody" Woodgeard, a former United States Marine from Ohio who studied with Onishi Kancho *Sensei* in Japan and helped promote the original *Koei-Kan Karate-Do* system.

These pioneers have profoundly shaped the course of the *Koei-Kan Karate-Do* system: past, present, and future. I feel deeply grateful to have the honor of being associated with people of this ilk.

Edward Kaloudis (Kaloudis *Sensei*) *Hanshi*/Eighth degree black belt *(Hachidan)*. United States Director and International Representative of *Koei-Kan Karate-Do.*

TABLE OF CONTENTS

PREFACE   *xi*

ACKNOWLEDGMENTS   *xiii*

INTRODUCTION   *xv*

1. THE MEANING OF KARATE   1

2. THE MEANING OF KOEI-KAN   3

3. BASIC HISTORICAL DEVELOPMENT OF KARATE   5

    India   5
    China   6
    Okinawa   8
    Japan   10

4. KOEI-KAN GENEALOGY—KEIZU   13

    Kushanku   13
    Takahara Peichin   13
    Sakugawa Tode   13
    Ruruko   14
    Matsumura Sokon   14
    Itosu Yasutsune   15
    Higaonna Kanryo   15
    Toyama Kanken   16
    Kyoda Juhatsu   16
    Kyo Kochi   18
    Onishi Eizo   18

5. BUDO (THE MARTIAL WAY) 21

Introduction	21
The Meaning of *Budo*	22
Basic Elements	23
Basic Principles and Axioms of *Budo*	31
The Middle Course	37
The Societal & Humanitarian Value of the *Budo*	38
Summary	40

6. THE DOJO (TRAINING HALL) 41

Background	41
Types of *Dojo*	42
Physical Characteristics of the *Dojo*	42
The Spirit of the Dojo	44
Historical Notes on the *Dojo*	44
Reigisaho and *Reishiki* (Etiquette and Ceremony)	44
Rei (Salutation or Bowing)	46
Soji (Cleaning the *Dojo*)	46
Structure of Seniority in the *Dojo*	47
Diagram of the *Dojo* (Training Area)	48

7. THE CLASS 51

Sensei (Teacher)	51
Keikogi (Practice Uniform)	51
Hakkai Shiki / Teuchi Shiki	
(Formal Class Opening and Closing Procedure)	52
Mokuso (Reflection or Meditation)	53
Taiso (Calisthenics)	54
Diagram of Formal Class Line-up	54
Renshu / Keiko (Training / Practice)	55
Outline of *Koei-Kan Karate-Do* Curriculum—*Kyoka*	56

8. TENSHIN WAZA (TECHNIQUES OF BODY TRANSFER)   59

9 KATA (FORM)   63

Areas of Performance   64
The Soul of Kata—*Katachi*   67
The Meaning of *Kata* Names   68
Training Hints   69
Notes on the Transmission of *Kata*   69
Notes on the Numeric Symbolism in *Kata* Names   70

10. BOGU (PROTECTIVE ARMOR)   71

11. EXAMINATION FOR RANK AND GRADE   73

A Brief Background of Rank and Grade   73
A Brief Background of Titles   74
Titles   75
Titles and Terms of Rank and Grade   75

12. HEIGO (MILITARY TERMINOLOGY)   79

General Terms   81
Useful Daily Expressions   82
Counting in Japanese   83
Fundamental Training Commands and Terms   84
Directional Terms   85
Contest *(Shiai)* Terms   86
Chart of Directions and Areas   86

13. MON AND MONSHO (CRESTS AND PATCHES)   89

14. HEIHO (STRATEGY)   91

15. KI, KIAI AND KIME (INTRINSIC ENERGY, SPIRIT LETTING AND FOCUS)   97

16. ANATOMY—KAIBOGAKU   99

General Parts of the Body   99
Basic Vital Areas of the Anatomy *(Kyusho)*   100

17. BASIC KINESIOLOGY AS APPLIED TO KARATE TECHNIQUES   103

Outline of Physical Techniques   104
A. Foundational Techniques   105
B. Primary Techniques   108
Uke Waza (Blocking Techniques)   108
Tsuki Waza (Punching Techniques)   109
Keri Waza (Kicking Techniques)   110
Uchi (or *Ate*) *Waza* (Striking Techniques)   112
C. Secondary Techniques   113
Nage No Kata (Throwing Methods)   113
Shime Waza (Choking Techniques)   115
Gyaku-Te (Joint Reversal Techniques)   116
Hazushi Waza (Escaping Techniques)   117
Basic Techniques—*Kihon Waza*
Random Sampling   119

In recent years the *Koei-Kan* system of *Karate-Do* has enjoyed continuous growth throughout various areas of the globe, although its fame is still limited to some extent. Quality as opposed to quantity has always been a general rule concerning the promulgation of *Koei-Kan*. This has perhaps been somewhat detrimental to a rapid expansion of the system, however, it has most certainly aided in the maintenance of high ideals and standards.

This book was written to serve as a brief introduction to the *Koei-Kan* system. It is by no means an in-depth treatise dealing with the totality of *Koei-Kan*, nor is it meant to be presented as a do-it-yourself manual. Rather, it is a source of information and reference concerning certain fundamental principles that are essential to the practice and study of this system.

It is hoped that this book will be useful as a supplement to one's personal training as well as an inspiration for continuous learning and improvement. Furthermore, it is the fervent desire of the author that this work will express the practical aspects of *Koei-Kan* while attempting to shed some amount of light on the ethical and philosophical principles that transcend the physiological, and will make this system (as well as *Karate-Do* in general and certain other martial entities) for some an entire lifestyle rather than merely a method of combat or exercise.

1. In Oriental languages it is customary to list the family name first and the surname last. Throughout this text this practice has been adhered to.
2. Throughout this text *Koei-Kan* is hyphenated, as is *Karate-Do*. It should be noted that *Koeikan*, *Karatedo*, etc., sans hyphen is also correct.

ACKNOWLEDGEMENTS

My Mother, the late Mrs. Elizabeth Frost, who typed much of the original notes for this text years ago and whose love and support have been invaluable. My Father, the late M. E. Frost, who instilled in me a fighting spirit at an early age. My senior pupil, Mr. Jack Sabat, who followed up on the completion of this work and whose loyalty has been constant. Ms. Jeanne Sheehan, who gave great encouragement and assistance and did the typing. Mr. Mark Scott for his valuable suggestions. Mr. Andy DeAngelis for his help in the compilation of the manuscript. Mr. Frank Jiordano for his help in translating certain characters from Japanese to Chinese. Mr. Jack Sabat, Dr. George Scordilis, Mr. Dave Spearing, Mr. Patrick Ciser, Mr. Jeff Mason, for their kind assistance in posing for the photographs. Mr. Hongo Naoki for his excellent calligraphy. Mr. Edward Kaloudis (my *Senpai),* Mr. Gary Clements, Mr. Richard Dine, and Mr. George Adrian, friends, brothers, and mentors all. All of my family, friends, and students who have supported my efforts throughout the years. My teacher, the venerable Master Onishi Eizo, who gave me substance and direction. Finally, to the way of *Karate,* to which I have devoted my entire existence. It has never let me down, although regrettably I have not always reciprocated in turn.

THE MEANING OF KARATE

Karate is formed by the combination of two Chinese ideograms, which may be literally translated as "empty hand." This translation is often construed to mean weaponless or unarmed, however, this definition is only partially correct. In order to better understand the true nature of Karate, it is important to examine these Chinese ideograms and others that have in the past been somehow related, for as Confucius stated in his analects known as the *Lun Yu,* "If the name is not correct, the words will not ring true." It should be noted that these Chinese ideograms, or characters known in Japanese as *Kanji,* are written the same in Japanese but pronounced differently in the spoken language.

Historically, many terms have been used to describe the fistic art that we know today as Karate. The most common of these are pronounced in Japanese: *Kenpo* (or *Kempo), Tode,* and *Te.* The terms *Kenpo* and *Tode* illustrate the close relationship that existed between Chinese fistic arts and those of Okinawa, which later evolved into Karate.

Kempo may be translated as "the way or law of the fist." *Kempo* is pronounced *Chuan Fa* in the Chinese Mandarin dialect and *Ken Fat* in the Cantonese dialect.

The character *To* used in writing *Tode* represents the famous Chinese T'ang Dynasty (618/906 A.D.), which had many effects of great consequence on Japan and Okinawa. The *To* ideogram may also be read as Kara which was at one time used to designate "China" or "things Chinese." The character used to symbolize the *De* in Tode simply means "hand," and it may also be pronounced *Te.*[1]

Te was often used as a shortened version of *Tode* to describe a fighting method that was practiced on Okinawa. When the *To* and *De* ideograms are combined they may roughly form a word meaning "China hand." *Tode* may also be pronounced *Karate,* however, this usage is different from the one that is commonly used at present. *Tode* (or *Karate)* was for the most part the standard method of describing the fistic art on Okinawa prior to 1906. At that time a book entitled *Karate Soshu Hen* was written by an Okinawan Karate expert named Hanashiro Chomo.[2]

In his book, Hanashiro replaced the *To* ideogram with one known as *Ku.*[3] When spoken, the *Ku* ideogram was still pronounced *Kara;* however, the meaning was not

The circle of nothingness = representing the cosmic void in Buddhist/Zen thought. This may be related to the Ku character used to represent the Kara (empty) in Karate taken from a Buddhist Sutra found in the book known as the "Hanya Shingyo" = "Shiki Soku Ye Ku, Ku Soku Ye Shiki." "Form becomes emptiness, emptiness becomes form." The circle may also represent peace (heiwa) or harmony (Wa), as found in the opening movement in the Kata Kushanku (Kusanku, Kosokun, Kwanku, Kanku, et al).

TO

TE

KU

TE

the same. The Kara that the *Ku* character represents may be translated as "empty" or "nothing." This is symbolic of a philosophical concept (generally originated in Buddhism) known in Japanese as *Mushin* or "nomindedness," where one is free of all thoughts that would hinder progression towards self improvement.

This connotation of "empty" indicates an attempt to show an ethical and philosophical value in Karate beyond the combative, physical element.

This change in the writing of Karate did not become the accepted form, however, until an Okinawan newspaper known as the *Ryukyu Shimpo Sha* arranged a gathering of certain prominent Okinawan Karate Masters in October of 1936 to review various elements of the art. Such notable experts as Yabu Kentsu, Kyan Chotoku, Motobu Choki, Miyagi Chojun, Kyoda Juhatsu, Chibana Choshin, Shiroma Shimpan, Hanashiro Chomo, and Soryoku Chotei met in the capital city of Naha and discussed topics that included the method to be used in the writing of Karate. It was decided that the *Ku* character was preferable to the older *To* ideogram due to its ethical connection, as well as to the fact that by abolishing the *To* character the implications of heavy Chinese influence would be greatly lessened. Soon after the conclusion of this meeting the use of the *Ku* character in the writing of Karate became the standard method and presently remains as such.

---

1. In the ancient Okinawan dialect (Hogen or Hogan) *Te* was commonly pronounced *Ti* or *Di*. Another early term used on Okinawa was *Bushi No Te* (Warrior *Te*).
2. Also known as Hanagi Chomo or Hanagusuku Chomo.
3. The *Ku* ideogram is taken from a Buddhist sutra found in a book known as the *Hanya Shingyo* (*Shiki Soku Ye Ku, Ku Soku Ye Shiki*). "Form becomes emptiness, emptiness becomes form."

THE MEANING OF KOEI-KAN

The name *Koei-Kan* was suggested to the founder of the system, Onishi Eizo, by his mentor, the late Master Toyama Kanken.

The fundamental translation of *Koei-Kan* from the Japanese is: happiness *(ko),* prosperity *(ei),* and hall or house *(kan).*

This definition is truly expressive of the nature and purpose of *Koei-Kan.*

To cultivate ourselves fully in an attempt to make the greatest use of our lives is the aim of *Koei-Kan* study. The development of this type of existence is beneficial to all life, as well as to that of the individual. The sentence "Prosper with happiness toward the future" has often been used to describe the mea ning of *Koei-Kan,* and it is mentioned here because it perhaps best exemplifies the intrinsic values of the *Koei-Kan* system.

KO

EI

KAN

Basic Historical Development of Karate

Various methods of individual combat "especially those of an unarmed nature" have been developed since the beginning of mankind. Systematic organization of these methods, however, did not occur quite so early. What we know today as Karate is of definite oriental lineage, although there is some evidence of occidental influence during the course of its development.

India

In India during pre-Christian times, there existed a warrior class known as the *Kshatriya*. This group was comparable to the Japanese Samurai. The *Kshatriya* were known to have practiced a fistic art called *Vajramushti,* which translates as "One whose clenched fist is adamant." The first recorded evidence of systemized Indian combat is found in the Buddhist work *The Lotus Sutra* (known as *Fa Hua San Ching* in Chinese and *Hokke-Kyo* in Japanese). In the Chinese version mention is made of a pugilistic form called *Hsiang Ch'a Hsiang P'u,* which means "mutual striking." In the Japanese edition, the same characters are used to represent the ancient wrestling form of Sumo.

The Lotus Sutra also refers to a combat method known as *Nata,* which means "a manly character, dancer, or performer." This form may be likened to the *Kata* currently used in Karate.

These arts are said to have been practiced by Buddhist monks of the period, however, there is little proof to substantiate this legend.

The link between martial art and spiritual philosophy played a tremendous role in forming present day systems such as Karate, although the original purposes of the two were far removed. Further evidence of fistic methods in ancient India is seen in the postures of certain Nio Bodhisattvas, which are statues of deities that are usually found outside Buddhist temples, supposedly guarding them. Replicas of these Nio guards can be found in Japan today at various temples. A widely believed theory traces the influence of Indian weaponless combat to China in the form of a Buddhist monk named Bodhidharma* (called Ta Mo in Chinese and Daruma Daishu, Dharma Taishi, or Daruma Taishi in Japanese).

Born in the small Indian province of Conjeeveram (also called Kanchipuram) south of Madras, Bodhitara (as he was originally named) was a member of the *Kshatriya* warrior caste and was trained in religious matters by a master of the Dhyana sect of Buddhism named Prajnatara, who gave his young disciple the name Bodhidharma. Through diligent study Bodhidharma became one of Prajnatara's chief pupils, and upon the death of his teacher Bodhidharma set out for China as a missionary to advance Buddhism.

CHINA

The three most credible records of information about Bodhidharma seem to differ on the date of his arrival in China. *Biographies of the High Priests,* written by the Chinese monk Tao Hsuan in 654 A.D. places Bodhidharma in China sometime during the Sung Dynasty (420–479 A.D., 420–589 A.D. of the Southern Dynasty), while the work called *Records of the Transmission of the Lamp,* written by the Priest Tao Yuan in 1000 A.D., indicates that Bodhidharma was in Canton province in 527 A.D., and the third source, *Records of the Lo-Yang Temple,* written by Yang Hsuan-Chih in 547 A.D. asserts that Bodhidharma was in Lo Yang in 520 A.D.

After examining all information, evidence points more specifically to the year 525 A.D. (or there about) as the date of Bodhidharma's arrival in China. The most significant information about Bodhidharma comes after his arrival at the famous Northern Shaolin-Ssu (Shaolin Monastery, pronounced *Shorin-Ji* in Japanese), located in the Honan province and known as the Sung Shan Shaolin-Ssu. Once there, Bodhidharma began developing and teaching his form of Buddhism, known in Chinese as Chan and in Japanese as Zen. This was based on the precepts of Dhyana, which he had studied in India. Seeing that the physical state of his students was not equal to the austere discipline of his teachings, he supposedly developed a series of physical exercises taken from watching various animals. The exercises were known in Chinese as the *Shih Pa Lo Han Sho (Ekkin Kyo* in Japanese), or "Eighteen Hands of the Lo Han" (Lo Han designates all famous followers of the original Buddha). The theory is that these eighteen drills were the foundation for the various Chinese fistic arts known collectively as *Chuan Fa* in Mandarin and *Kung Fu* or *Gung Fu* in Cantonese. Bodhidharma,' eighteen exercises were eventually spread by his Shaolin-Ssu disciples.

---

*The name Bodhidharma designates one who has deeply penetrated (Bodhi) religion and Buddhist laws and principles (Dharma).

It was also at the Honan Shaolin that Bodhidharma allegedly sat facing a wall in meditation for nine years. The art developed by Bodhidharma was purported to have been recorded in two books that he wrote. One, entitled *Hsi Sui Chin*, has since been lost, and the other, known as the *I-Chin Ching*, has been proven to be forgery written during the nineteenth century, hundreds of years following the death of Bodhidharma.

Several decades after Bodhidharma's death in 534 A.D., a fistic arts expert named Ch'ueh Yuan Sang-Jen supposedly travelled to the Shensi province where he, along with another Chinese martial arts master named Li, originated 152 additional techniques. They combined them with the original eighteen to form a total of 170, to which they gave names such as "dragon," "snake," "tiger," "crane," "monkey," and "leopard." The weaponless types of combat that were developed from the Honan Shaolin may be termed *Wai Chia* (external, outer, or hard school) and encompass eight distinctive systems, known as *Hung Chuan, T'ei Yu Tan Tui, Hon Chuan, Erh-Lang Men, Fan Chuan, Ch'a Chuan, Mi Tsung Yi,* and *Pa Chuan*.

The first two systems are attributed to the Sung Dynasty (1127–1279 A.D.) the next four to the Ming dynasty (1368–1644 A.D.) and the last two are of the Ching period (1644–1911 A.D.). Each of these methods have a great many branches at the present time.

Under the *Wai Chia* category there is also the southern Shaolin-Ssu, known as the Chuan Chow Shaolin-Ssu which is located in Fukien Province. Within the structure of the southern Shaolin there are six major groups, each with a wide variety of styles. The six groups are the *Ta Hung Men, Liu-Chia Chuan, Ts'ai-Chia Chuan, Mo-Chia Chuan, Kwantung,* and *Fukien*. All branches of the *Wai Chia* may be broken into three vast groups: the *Hung,* or hard; the *Kung* or soft; and the *Yue,* or hard and soft.

The *Neh Chia* (inner or soft school) was formed subsequent to the *Wai Chia* and is thought to have been founded by a Chinese master named Chang Sen Feng, a Taoist monk. This theory is lacking in legitimate historical proof. The *Neh Chia* has six divisions and each of these have many sub-divisions. The six divisions are the *Hsing I Chuan, Pa Kua Chuan, Tai Chi Chuan, Wu Tang Pai, Tzu Jan Men,* and *Liu He Pa Fa*.

The *Neh Chia* and the *Wai Chia* are the two representative forms of all Chinese *Chuan Fa* and literally all Chinese Wu-Shu (a general term which is used to describe all martial arts including systems of weaponry). There is one source that believes *Chuan Fa* sprang up during the Han dynasty (209 B.C.–24 A.D.), and another states that it began five thousand years ago during the reign of Emperor Huang-Ti; however, there is not enough conclusive evidence to validate these two theories.

As time went on *Chuan Fa* was developed and taught in relative secrecy. A great deal of *Chuan Fa's* growth was due to its promotion through religious sects and Tong societies. At present there are literally hundreds of Chinese *Chuan Fa* type arts being practiced throughout the world.

OKINAWA

The next important historical step in the transmission and propagation of oriental fistic art leads to Okinawa, the main island of the Ryukyu chain (formerly known by their Chinese name of the Liu-Chiu's, or Luchuans). The word Okinawa means "rope in the offing," and it was here that astronomical changes were made that helped bring about Karate's present appearance.

GATHERING OF FAMOUS OKINAWAN MASTERS.
(Standing, left to right) Shiroma Shinpan (Shinpei), Chitose Tsuyoshi (Gochoku), Chibana Choshin, Nakasone Genwa.
(Seated, left to right) Kyan (Kyabu) Chotoku, Yabe (Yabu) Kentsu, Hanashiro (Hanagusuku / Hanagi) Chomo, Miyagi (Miyagusuku) Chojun.

The Okinawans, it seems, had their own method of unarmed self defense prior to their contact with China. This method was called Tode, a name which was later used to specify the fistic style representative of the city of Naha.

It is commonly supposed that Chinese *Chuan Fa* found its way to Okinawa during China's T'ang dynasty through Chinese expeditions at that time. In 1372 A.D., during the Ming era, King Satto of Okinawa openly welcomed communications with China's Emperor Hung Wu-Ti. From this point relations rapidly increased. Sometime during the Ming dynasty, a settlement composed of Okinawans formed in the Chinese capital of Chuan-Chou. Okinawans who traveled back and forth between China and Okinawa imported many things, including, possibly fistic art.

In 1392 A.D. Chinese pilgrims came to Okinawa and established a Chinese community. This community has been historically called the "thirtysix families." *Chuan Fa* experts were believed to have been included among the ranks of this settlement; this being the case, Chinese fistic art was further bolstered and integrated. In 1429 A.D. (during the Okinawan Sho era) King Hashi Sho brought about the unification of Okinawa's three major territories of Hokuzan, Nanzan, and Chuzan. These names were later changed to *Kunigami, Shimajiri,* and *Nakagami* respectively.

Under King Hashi's rule, trade with Indochina was encouraged and, it appears, pugilistic styles from this area were imported, thereby exposing Okinawa to yet another faction of combat.

During his reign, King Hashi prohibited the common people from bearing arms. This step undoubtedly aided in the promotion of fistic methods of combat. A great turning point for Okinawa and specifically unarmed combative development occurred in 1609 A.D., following Japan's civil war between the Tokugawa and Satsuma factions in 1600 A.D. The Tokugawa clan was victorious; the defeated Satsuma clan (from Japan's southern-most island, Kyushu), seeking further adventure, attacked and conquered their neighbor to the south, Okinawa.

Under the rule of Shimazu Iehisa, the Satsuma leader, the Okinawans were dealt with severely, and stricter weapons control was enforced. This situation forced the Okinawans to pursue self defense methods more thoroughly. The various pugilistic groups began to form and develop their only remaining weapons, which consisted of certain farm implements and their hands and feet. It was under these circumstances that pugilism was practiced and advanced in secrecy. Ideas and theories were exchanged by these Okinawan secret societies and, in the early seventeenth century, this exchange produced a fighting style that was termed *Okinawa-Te* or simply *Te* (hand). The main purpose of *Te* at that time was to injure or kill. The utmost secrecy continued to shroud the practice of *Te*, which was openly displayed only during actual combat.

As time went on the cities of Shuri, Naha, and Tomari were established as the major centers of *Te* development, and from these fountainheads systemization sprouted. Okinawans began to put more emphasis on individualism in their methods so that they would be able to perform techniques unknown to others. These methods were closely guarded and tested only during duels.

In the following years teachers of Chinese fistic art came to Okinawa in growing numbers to teach. Military and political attaches (as well as others) instructed various groups of Okinawans, who in turn continued to disseminate these methods. The next important development came about when *Te* separated into three vast schools, each with certain identifiable characteristics. This development took place in the cities of Shuri, Naha, and Tomari. The word *Te* was added as a suffix to the name of each city, which classified the three schools into *Shuri-Te, Naha-Te, Tomari-Te.* As progress continued the *Shuri-Te* and *Naha-Te* methods became dominant.

JAPAN

There is great evidence that Chinese fistic arts reached Japan and were, to some extent, transmitted and combined with various indigenous forms long before the Okinawan methods were introduced there. However, it was not until 1922 that Karate was brought from Okinawa to Japan on a permanent and public basis. At this

time an Okinawan Karate expert named Gichin Funakoshi traveled to Tokyo to give a demonstration of Karate at Japan's First National Athletic Exhibition. Shortly thereafter, Mr. Funakoshi journeyed to various areas of Japan introducing Karate, and as a result he established a Dojo. Later he taught at various universities and clubs throughout the country.

In subsequent years other Okinawan Karate experts such as Miyagi

Master Kyoda Juhatsu as a young man (left) with his teacher, Master Higaonna (Higashionna) Kanryo.

Chojun, Mabuni Kenwa, Toyama Kanken, Kyoda Juhatsu went to Japan to teach
and/or demonstrate their methods to the general populace.

In this fashion Karate was firmly planted in Japan, where it has been continu-
ously researched and practiced.

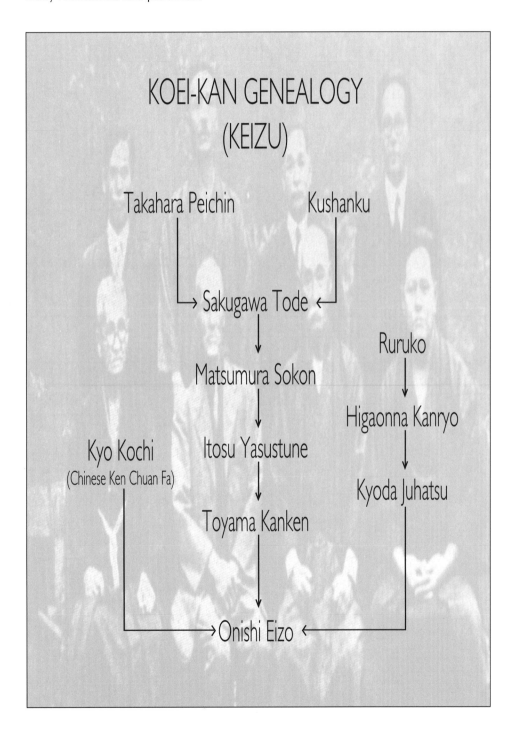

4

4

Koei-Kan Genealogy

Keizu

Kushanku

Also known as Kusankun, Kusanku, Kuanku, Kosokun or Koshankun (Kung Kong Su or Kung Hsiang Chun in Chinese), Kushanku was a military attache from China, skilled in fistic arts, who was sent to Okinawa sometime in the mid to late 1700s. It is believed that he was accompanied by an Okinawan from Shuri by the name of Shionja who trained with him in China. This incident was recorded in a book entitled *Oshima Hikki,* written by Tobe Ryoen of Tosa village, Okinawa. Kushanku is credited with the creation of the *Kata* bearing his name. His most notable pupil was Sakugawa Tode.

Takahara Peichin

Takahara Peichin was an Okinawan teacher of Karate from Akata village who was well known as an astronomer and mapmaker. His most noteworthy pupil was Sakugawa Tode.

Sakugawa Tode (1733–1815)

Born Kanga Teruya in Tori Hori village in Shuri, Okinawa, Sakugawa Tode (also known as Sakuma Tode or Sakugawa Chikudoun Peichin) was a security officer for a commercial shipping line who began his training under Takahara Peichin and later studied with the famous Chinese military attache Kushanku.

Tode was the early Okinawan word for Karate and was given to Sakugawa for his skill in the fistic art. He was perhaps the most influential figure in the early development of Okinawan Karate. Sakugawa Tode is credited with establishing an early code or set of precepts known as the *Dojo Kun:* Seek perfection of character *(Jinkaku No Tassei).* Be faithful *(Seijitsude Are).* Endeavor to excel *(Kojoshin Wo Mote).* Respect others *(Tanin Wo Uyamae).* Refrain from violent behavior *(Mizukarano Chikara Wo Seigyoseyo).*

His most noteworthy pupils were Matsumura Sokon and Matsumoto.

RURUKO

Ruruko, also known as Ryuru Ko, Ryu Ryo, Ryu Ryo Ko, and Liu Liu Kung (in Chinese), was a Chinese teacher of a form of southern Shaolin *Chuan Fa* (known as *Nakitsuru Ken* in Japanese) based in Fuzhou in the province of Fukien. He worked as a carpenter and is best known as the instructor of Master Higaonna Kanryo during Higaonna's stay in China. Ruruko taught Master Higaonna the five forms *(Kata)* that became the foundation of Okinawan *Naha-te: Sanchin, Seisan, Sanseiru, Seipai* and *Suparinpei.*

MATSUMURA SOKON (1809–1901)

Matsumura Sokon (also known as Matsumura Bushi, Matsumura Bucho, Matsumura Buseitatsu, or Matsumura Unyu) was born in the Yamagawa village in Shuri, Okinawa. He studied under Sakugawa Tode and, to a lesser degree, the Chinese military attaches Iwah and Ason.

Matsumura served as an instructor and bodyguard to the last three Okinawan kings: Sho Ko, Sho Iku, and Sho Tai. He also served as an envoy for the Okinawan royal family, and as such, travelled to Fuzhou in Fukien province, where he studied Chinese fistic arts. Matsumura was given the title *Bushi* or Warrior which was a title of great respect given to a select few who possessed superior ability in the martial arts.

Among his most notable pupils were Itosu Yasustune, Kuwae Ryosei, Yabu Kentsu (Yabe Norimichi), Kyan (Kyabu), Azato Yasustune and Hanagi (Hanashiro) Chomo (Hanagusuku Nagashige).

ITOSU YASUSTUNE (1830–1915)

Itosu Yasustune (also known as Itosu Anko and Shishu An) was born at Yamagawa Village in Shuri, Okinawa. He was (along with Higaonna Kanryo) one of the two major fountainheads in the development of modern era Okinawan Karate.

Itosu began his training under Matsumura Sokon and became his top pupil. He also trained to some degree with Gusukuma and Matsumora Kosaku of Tomari. Itosu was a short, stocky man who possessed great strength. He could reportedly crush stalks of bamboo in his bare hand, and he was known for his skill in the *Naihanchin Kata*.

Master Itosu introduced Karate to the Okinawan school system as part of a physical education program at the Shuri Jinjo Elementary School and the Dai Ichi Junior High School. He also served as an instructor to the Okinawan Royal Family.

Perhaps of all Okinawan Karate teachers Master Itosu had the most distinguished list of pupils, including Funakoshi Gichin, Chibana Choshin, Hanashiro Chomo, Mabuni Kenwa, Yabu Kentsu, Tokuda Anbun, Toyama Kanken, Yabiku Moden and Shiroma Shimpan.

HIGAONNA KANRYO (1852–1915)

Higaonna Kanryo (also known as Higashionna Kanryo and nicknamed "Machu," or "Moshi," as a child) was born in Nishimura Village in Naha, Okinawa. He, along with Itosu Yasustune was one of the two major fountainheads in the development of modern era Okinawan Karate.

It is believed that Higaonna first received instruction in Tode from an Okinawan named Arakaki Seisho from Kume Village, Naha. At the age of twenty he travelled to Fuzhou province in Fukien, China, with a fellow Okinawan named Yoshimura Udon. Upon arriving, he stayed at an Okinawan settlement called Ryukyukan and soon after made the acquaintance of a Chinese martial arts expert named Ruruko, from whom he learned a southern Shaolin form of *Chuan Fa* (known as *Nakitsuru Ken* in the Japanese pronunciation).

After fifteen years in China, Higaonna returned to Okinawa, where he became a martial arts instructor for the Royal Family during the reign of King Sho Tai.

Master Higaonna was well known for his ability in the *Kata Sanchin*. His main disciples were Kyoda Juhatsu, Miyagi Chojun, and to a lesser degree, Mabuni Kenwa.

Master Toyama (Oyadomari) Kanken

TOYAMA KANKEN (1888–1966)

Toyama Kanken (also known as Oyadomari Kanken) was born on September 24th in Shuri, Okinawa, where he studied under and became a senior student of Master Itosu Yasutsune. He also trained to a lesser degree with Master Higaonna Kanryo and a Master Itarashiki. Toyama rounded out his martial arts studies by learning traditional Okinawan weapons *(Kobudo)* under Masters Oshiro, Chibana, and Tani.

Master Toyama moved to Taiwan in 1924, where he took a position as an elementary school principal. During this period he studied Chinese fistic arts under Masters Chin and Rin. In 1930 he moved to the Meguro section of Tokyo where he established his Dojo, which he named Shudokan.

Toyama founded the All Japan Karate-Do Association *(Zen Nihon Karate-Do Renmei)* in 1946. Master Toyama taught many noteworthy pupils, both through the Shudokan and through the auspices of the All Japan Karate-Do Association.

KYODA JUHATSU (1888–1967)

Kyoda Juhatsu was born in the city of Naha, Okinawa. He began his karate training under Higaonna Kanryo at the age of fifteen, one month before Miyagi (Miyagusuku) Chojun (1888–1953), the founder of *Goju Ryu,* began his training.

Kyoda was a middle school teacher and principal who established several karate programs within the Okinawan school system. He served for a period as the chief Karate instructor for the Okinawan branch of the Dai Nippon Butokukai Kai during the 1930s.

Master Kyoda called his system *To-On Ryu* after the Japanese characters that represented the name of his teacher, Higaonna.

In 1944 he moved to the city Beppu (Oita Prefecture) on the island of Kyushu where he taught a limited number of select pupils. During his later years his eldest son, Juko, took on the majority of his teaching responsibilities. Master Kyoda was well known for his expertise in the *Kata Sanseiru.*

Master Toyama (Oyadomari) Kanken seated right. Master Onishi Eizo standing, black Uwagi (jacket).

Master Kyoda Juhatsu

Mr. Onishi Yukinaga (Onishi Kancho's father second from left), Master Toyama (Oyadomari) Kanken, Master Onishi Eizo

KYO KOCHI

Master Kyo Kochi (pronounced Shue Sheng Zhi in Chinese) was a professor at the Taiwan Medical University. Master Kyo was an expert in Chinese medicine as well as an expert in a variety of Chinese martial arts.

ONISHI EIZO

Known as Kancho *Sensei* to his followers, Master Onishi was born in Iyo-Gun village in the Ehime-Ken prefecture on the island of Shikoku, Japan. As a descendant of the Oshimiki Samurai clan, he was initiated into the martial arts and ways at an early age. He received his introduction to Karate from an Okinawan teacher, Shimabukuro Shigehiko, and later became the leading disciple of the famed Master Toyama Kanken.

Onishi Kancho Sensei obtained a letter of introduction from Master Toyama to another renowned Okinawan Master, Kyoda Juhatsu, and was eventually accepted as his pupil. In this fashion Master Onishi became thoroughly schooled in both

Shuri-Te and *Naha-Te*. Onishi Kancho Sensei began teaching at the Iyo Shrine in 1951. Shortly thereafter he gave instruction to the Karate clubs of the Matsuyama Foreign Language College, Ehime University and Kochi University. In 1952, Master Onishi, with the advice and consent of Masters Toyama and Kyoda, established *Koei-Kan,* and on April 2, 1954, he opened the first official Dojo in the Kanagawa prefecture.

During this period he was residing at the headquarters *(Honbu)* of the All-Japan Karate-Do Association in the Meguro section of Tokyo when Master Toyama received a request from the U.S. Air Force to make a documentary film on Karate. Master Toyama accepted, and assigned Onishi Kancho along with another instructor, Mr. Ikeda Yukimitsu, to demonstrate. As a result, Master Onishi began teaching U.S. military officers in the Yoyogi section of Tokyo. He furthered his knowledge by becoming a pupil of a Chinese Master named Kyo Kochi (Japanese pronunciation) in 1957,

Master Onishi Eizo

and later studied andexchanged ideas with another Chinese Master named An Tenei (Japanese pronunciation). In this capacity Master Onishi has travelled to mainland China and Taiwan. Master Onishi succeeded Master Toyama as Chairman of the All-Japan Karate-Do Association, and in 1975 he crystallized the formation of a separate curriculum, which he termed *Karate-Do Gaku* and later *Kendo Gaku (Ken*—fist, *Do*—way, *Gaku*—study).

Onishi *Kancho Sensei* has taught throughout Asia, North America, South America, and Europe. Master Onishi currently serves as the Chairman of the International Koei-Kan Karate-Do Federation and the International Kendo Gaku Federation (with Headquarters in Tokyo, Japan). Master Onishi has authored five books in Japanese and continues to teach and lecture worldwide.

FOOTNOTE

Many of the names listed in the genealogy are given in both the Japanese pronunciation and in the ancient Okinawan dialect known as Hogan. In some cases there is more than one name listed for the same person. These are either nicknames, name changes, which were a common practice on Okinawa, or different pronunciations of the same characters.

It should be further noted as a point of reference that the Okinawan people are referred to in *Hogan* as *Uchinanchu*. The title *Peichin* describes a class of Okinawan officials who were responsible for civil law enforcement and administration. There were two classifications of *Peichin: Chikudun,* recruited from the common people, and *Satunushi,* recruited from the upper class. The *Peichin* were extant from 1509 to 1879.

5

BUDO

THE MARTIAL WAY

INTRODUCTION

The martial way *(Budo)* connotes the philosophical, moral, and ethical principles that are at the heart of the martial arts *(Bujutsu,* or *Bugei)*.

The original aim of martial arts practice was the practical development of combative skills for use in life and death struggles. As such, expedience and efficiency were of prime concern. Fast and effective techniques were imperative to survival. The strong emphasis placed upon cultivating deadly combative techniques (in the case of the *Bujutsu)* versus the building of an admirable character through the cultivation of a sound philosophy, a correct sense of morality, and a constructive code of ethics (as in the *Budo),* is often cited as the basic difference between the two. It must, however, be stated that the Samurai of old rigidly adhered to a code known as *Bushido* (the way of the warrior), which primarily dealt with proper ritualistic conduct and etiquette *(Reishiki/Reigisaho),* duty and obligation *(Giri),*and honor *(Meiyo).* By the same token the Budo should not be mistakenly thought of as being concerned with character development to the exclusion of combative efficiency. The two areas must be synergistic for optimal results; ergo practical and effective technique is of the utmost importance to the practice of the *Budo.*

Philosophy: "The love and pursuit of knowledge and wisdom. Inquiry into the nature of things based on logical reasoning."

Morals: "Of or concerned with the judgement of the goodness or badness of human action and character."

Ethics: "A set of principles of right conduct."

These three elements are paramount to the study and practice of the martial way. The philosophy of the *Budo* has been influenced by the teachings of Confucius (Kung Tsu in Chinese, Koshi in Japanese) and the Chinese sage Lao Tzu (Roshi in

Japanese) as found in their written works *Lun Yu* (Analects) and *Tao Te Ching* ("The Book of the Way and its Virtue"), respectively. Other influences may be found in the teachings of Mencius (Meng Tse in Chinese, Moshi in Japanese), Buddhism, Shintoism, Zen (much through the teachings of the Zen priest Takuan), the afore-mentioned code of *Bushido,* the text of *Sun Tzu* ("The Art of War"), and the individual thoughts and philosophies of martial arts masters both past and present.

The *Budo* is not a religion. It is compatible with all modes of constructive and positive thoughts, actions and values. The major aims of the *Budo* are to foster a unity of mind, body, and spirit and to promote a happy, healthy, and prosperous life. It is important to realize that the essence of the martial arts and ways can only be reached through training and practice. This is known in Japanese as *Isshin Denshin* (nonverbal understanding and transmission). One must learn through experience, i.e., by doing.

Finally the *Budo* emphasizes the positive cultivation of our individuality towards the betterment and furtherance of our lives but never at the expense of others. "Do unto others as you would have others do unto you."

THE MEANING OF BUDO

BU

HOKO

TOMARU

According to Kenkyusha's *New Japanese English Dictionary* the word Budo means military (martial) arts, military science, the precepts of the Samurai, and chivalry. However, upon closer examination we find that *Budo* goes far beyond such a superficial (and to some extent erroneous) definition.

The word Budo is made up of two Chinese ideograms. The first ideogram, which represents *Bu* in the word *Budo,* is comprised of two sub-ideograms (radicals). The sub-ideogram that makes up the upper and right hand portions represents the Japanese word *Hoko,* which is a spear or halberd used originally in ancient times by the Chinese, who called it *Ko.* The second sub-ideogram, which completes the character *Bu,* is comprised of the lower and left hand portion, which symbolizes the Japanese word *Tomaru* (to "stop" or "end").

After combining these two sub-ideograms we have roughly "To Stop A Spear." In a broader sense the character representative of *Bu* may be interpreted as the quelling of violence or a halt to strife and fighting. Ultimately we may define Bu as peace.

DO

Words such as "strong," "warrior," "tactics," and "fierce" are also associated with *Bu,* showing a firm connection with martial systems.

The Chinese character that represents the *Do* in Budo (known as *Michi* as well as *Do* in Japanese, and as *Tao* pronounced *Dao* in Chinese) is also made up of two sub-ideograms. The first part has through the years experienced various changes and interpretations of its meaning. These meanings may be fundamentally grouped to form "moving feet at a crossroads." The second part of *Do* is a phonetic symbol that is a homonym for "step."

Prior to the use of Chinese characters in Japan, the Japanese applied the word *Chi* to designate a road or path. This was prefixed by *Mi* which denoted "sacred" because it was commonly believed that all roads were under the care of deities.

The Chinese character that represents *Tao* or *Do* is a closely connected principle in such profound philosophies as Taoism and Confucianism.

The philosopher Lao Tsu, who originated Taoism during the Chinese period of "Warring States" (403 B.C.–221 B.C.), referred to *Tao* in his book, *Tao Te Ching.* In this reference he stated: "There is a thing confusedly formed, born before heaven and earth, silent and void, standing alone and unchanging, moving everywhere but never tiring, capable of being the mother of the world; I know not its name, but I will call it Tao. The Tao is the reversal of all things, neither being nor nonbeing, neither the nameless nor the named, neither the concrete nor the abstract. It is an uncarved block, absolute simplicity which contains within it the potential for the myriad universe."

Although this character was originally linked with words that were related to roads or paths, it has been widely used to convey a sense of proper moral and ethical conduct. The usage of Do in this fashion reflects a course one follows in life as a means toward an end, thus representing the constant process of improvement in an effort to unify oneself.

This character is commonly found in Japanese words that pertain to moral, philosophical and ethical conduct, such as *Jindo* (way of harmony), *Dori* (way of logic), *Dotoku* (way of virtue), and *Dogi* (way of justice). It is for these reasons that Do is the suffix used in describing the martial ways or philosophies (e.g. Kendo, Judo, Karate-Do, Aikido etc.) for it reflects the "Way," "Road," "Path," or "Course" that one follows or takes in life.

BASIC ELEMENTS

Through the years *Budo* has evolved into a total life philosophy, which endears and propagates such qualities as humility, truth, self-discipline, self-Reliance, peace, respect, unselfishness, honor, courage, loyalty and perseverance.

The cultivation of mind, body, and spirit to form a harmonious being is an important aim of *Budo.* To be as one with oneself allows oneness with all to be achieved. Knowledge and understanding of self allows knowledge and understanding of others.

The *Budo-Ka* (practitioner of *Budo)* does not believe in a total perfection, yet he constantly seeks it. In this respect he is likened to a mountain climber who attempts to scale a peakless mountain. He cannot see the peak yet he continues to climb higher. The importance lies in the climb. The reaching of greater heights. So it is in *Budo* that the importance lies in one's continuous improvement and cultivation. The constant seeking of greater levels. This concept is often very difficult to grasp for man has a tendency to look at things strictly on a beginning and an end basis. When one cannot see an end to something he often feels his efforts are futile and gives up in frustration. It is for this reason that a *Budo-Ka* must look beyond the superficial to the real. In order to view things on a real basis one must obtain a state of mind known in Japanese as *Mushin* (nomindedness). This means a pure, free, uncluttered mind that is capable of adapting to all circumstances, just as water shapes itself to all vessels that contain it.

In a work known as *Fudochishinmyoroku* (The Mysterious Record of Immovable Wisdom), a famous Japanese priest of the Zen sect of Buddhism named Takuan Soho (1573–1645) attempts to explain a proper *Budo* state of mind to a highly regarded fencer of the day named Yagyu Tajima No Kami by saying "The pure, inborn mind is the real mind as opposed to the worldly or false mind, which has become cluttered and soiled through life experiences. *Budo* intends to restore the original purity of the mind as it was at birth. In so doing the mind becomes calm, as a pool of clear, undisturbed water from which all objects may be reflected." This principle is known in Japanese as *Mizu No Kokoro* ("A mind like water").

The physical manifestations of Budo are the techniques *(Waza)* that act as the vehicles for its transmission. Without these vehicles *Budo* would not exist. The early evolution of *Budo* was influenced by such Eastern philosophies as *Bukkyo* (Buddhism), *Dokyo* (Confucianism) and *Jukyo* (Taoism). As *Budo* progressed this influence became more philosophical than theological.

One philosophy that is greatly absorbed in Budo is that of Zen. Zen should not be considered Zenshu or Zen Buddhism, because while the two are similar, they are not the same. Zenshu is merely a sect which came into being after the death of Siddhartha the Buddha. The traditional founder of this sect was Boddhidharma (mentioned in the section on the historical development of Karate).

Zen is a contraction of the Sanskrit word *Zen-No,* which means "Silent Meditation" *(Jo-Ryo* in Japanese). It propagates a state of mind free from all desires of the world and is concerned with examination and improvement of self. A form of Zen was practiced in India by Brahmins long before the birth of Buddha. Along with freeing oneself from desires, Zen aims at controlling the emotions.

These areas are extremely important in *Budo* and aid in enabling one to perceive a complete tranquility, which leads to the ultimate state of enlightenment, known as *Satori* in Japanese. *Budo* embodies these precepts as well as the value placed on meditation and contemplation. This type of reflection may be termed *Mokuso* in the martial ways and is actually a method of *Za-Zen* (seated meditation), which is heavily stressed. Various postures are used for meditation, and breathing is generally of a deep, relaxed, abdominal nature. While the *Budo* philosophy is far reaching, a firm understanding may be obtained through examining some of the laudable qualities propounded in *Budo*.

KENSON ➤ Humility

The quality of humility is too often confused with subservience, which is definitely not the case in the *Budo* philosophy. True humility is born from the knowledge and belief that all human beings are at the most basic level deserving of consideration.

Humility is the manifestation of self-confidence and respect. The knowledge of one's own capabilities and limitations, and the inner security that eliminates the need for one to prove superiority over another. The more prowess one holds in a particular field, the more this person will come to understand the futility of boasting in word or deed, for true ability is readily seen and needs no aggrandizement. There is a famous oriental saying that tells us "The more fruit the rice stalk bears, the lower in bows." When a human being comes to realize the immensity of life, the significance of the individual comes to seem less important and the worth of human beings collectively is elevated to its true position.

Budo teaches that the value of others as well as ourselves must be understood and accepted so that a truly humble attitude may be cultivated.

SHINRI ➤ Truth

Truth is the quintessence of reality. Reality is the basis of all meaningful examination and subsequent formation of thought and theory. In *Budo* it is believed that no decisive progress can be made without honest evaluation.

Reality oriented knowledge is the guiding factor in the course of human life. The expansion of one's learning in an attempt to free the mind from its limitations and to achieve an open state of thought should be regarded as a primary objective, since it is knowledge which aids in effecting correct judgement.

Shakespeare wrote in *Henry VI* (act IV, scene 7) that "Ignorance is the curse of God/Knowledge the wing wherewith we fly to heaven." Intrinsic (fundamental or basic) knowledge cannot be grasped if one views things falsely, ergo, the necessity of truth, the recognition of reality. Things are often not what they would seem to be and the wrong path may be followed if one is not honest with oneself. In dealing with others, honesty is imperative lest they be influenced for the worse. A *Budo-Ka* must seek the essence of things and define the facts of reality in order to go beyond the superficial. There is a famous oriental fable that relates the experience of three blind men who had never gazed upon an elephant.

One day, each of the blind men had occasion to touch an elephant. The first felt the trunk and reasoned that an elephant must be like a snake. The second touched the elephant's side and thought an elephant was the same as a wall. Finally the third blind man felt the leg and was certain an elephant was like a tree.

The constant search for truth avoids the mistake of grasping only superficial knowledge and allows us to understand Aristotle's law of identity, that things are what they are. This in turn leads toward enlightenment.

KUNREN ➤ Self Discipline / Effort

The key to continual improvement lies in one's mastery of discipline (of self) on virtually all levels of life. To surpass the boundaries of what would appear to be the limits of mind and body leads to a spiritual fortitude that is capable of weathering the storms of severe adversity. The ability to control emotions is perhaps the most difficult part of self-reliance.

The feelings of joy, anger, happiness, sorrow, love, and hate effect and guide the life of the individual as well as the lives of those in immediate contact with said individual, and society in general. This affect can be truly immense. As human beings we are motivated by our desires. These desires are often of a selfish nature and tend to lead us away from basic goals of advancement and betterment for the benefit of mankind.

The desire of fame, fortune, and power sways many to a course of impropriety, which easily becomes destructive.

The Chinese philosopher Lao-Tzu stated that "Freedom from desire leads to inward peace." The attempt must be made to overcome ourselves through the constant training of the mind, body, and spirit in an austere manner. We must set aside laziness, despondency, self-pity, and the attitude of unconcern so that we may rise to new heights rather than stagnate.

This challenge originates from oneself to oneself, and it must be met. It is a natural attitude for one to cast blame elsewhere when things don't develop to one's personal satisfaction. Such negative thoughts only hinder progress.

Self-reliance is an important part of discipline. The chief responsibility for a human being's future, happiness and prosperity rests in the hands of the individual. The ability to cope with all forms of adversity must be developed on a physical, psychological, and spiritual basis. Standing on one's own two feet and following the course in life that is chosen requires a great deal of self-reliance, self-confidence and individuality if we are to obtain our goals without doing so at the expense of others.

This can only be fulfilled when one accepts and correctly uses positive individuality. It should also be kept in mind that the wind belongs to those who set their sails, and only through diligent effort and discipline from within ourselves can we reap the benefits that we all have the potential to obtain.

WA ➤ Peace / Harmony

Peace/Harmony is the very essence of *Budo*. For this reason the indiscriminate use of force and violence is eschewed by the *Budo-Ka*. This attitude should not be misconstrued as a passive acceptance of injustice, for *Budo* holds dear the concept of justice. To be in harmony with all things is achieved only through a deep reverence for peace.

At times, however, peace is regrettably realized only through the use of strength as a reinforcement to a just and morally right cause. On such occasions the only recourse one has is to act according to the situation in an attempt to restore, preserve, and further a state of peace.

Conflict, violence, and discord are commonplace states in life and breed hatred, mistrust, disunity, fear and sorrow. In order to attain the total fulfillment of human potentialities one must seek a peace within oneself and with all others. Physical preparedness is essential to this goal, but the use of strength and combative skill are resorted to only as a final step.

In the Chinese martial classic of the Chou Dynasty, *The Art of War,* it is written that "The ultimate good lies not in winning a hundred battles, but in overcoming a man or an enemy without a conflict." This is surely a goal of high merit and it is an undertaking worthy of great pains. However, a prerequisite to a true state of peace is self-confidence. This enables a person to have a greater understanding of self and makes one more readily capable of understanding others.

Budo—"To stop a spear." In essence, to stop conflict. Ultimately, peace. Inner peace as well as peace with all around us.

Through austere training we forge the mind, body, and spirit into a strong, focused, unified individual capable of dealing with and adapting to all situations. This leads to self confidence, self reliance and a sense of well-being that allows us to deal with others in a secure fashion. There is no true peace or justice without strength.

Theodore Roosevelt (1858–1919), the twenty-sixth president of the United States wrote "Speak softly, but carry a big stick." This attitude is embodied in the Latin phrase *qui desiderat pacem praeparet bellum,* or "Let him who desires peace, prepare for war." It is stated that "the sharpest sword is never drawn." One who has developed skill in the *Budo* exudes an aura that in most cases precludes aggressive behavior on the part of others. There are, however, exceptions to this rule, in which case the well trained *Budo-Ka* (practitioner of Budo) is prepared to take appropriate actions. In this fashion we may truly find the Wa (peace/harmony) as connoted in *Budo.*

SONKEI ➤ Respect

Respect is imperative to human progression and peace. A state of harmony cannot exist unless consideration is given to society, nature, and individuals. On an individual level, respect is earned through conduct. Confucius (known in Chinese as Kung-Ts and in Japanese as Koshi) stated that "The good man does not grieve that other people do not recognize his merits. His only anxiety is lest he should fail to recognize theirs."

Respect begins with self-respect. Through constant examination and cultivation of ourselves we may gain a sense of self-respect, which is a fundamental step toward developing a feeling of respect for humanity in general.

An oriental proverb that expresses the *Budo* idea of respect tells us that "The mountain does not laugh at the river because it is lowly, nor does the river speak ill of the mountain because it cannot move about." Each has a purpose and each plays a significant role in the total scheme of life.

HI RIKO SHUGI ➤ Unselfishness

In the *Budo* the quality of being unselfish is considered an admirable virtue. A monk called Soshi made the point in his writings that "Men of poor character are greedy and seek fame and fortune even at the expense of others. The sage would, if the need arises, lay down his life for his country."

This is not merely a statement of nationalism, but rather it means that the person of high moral and ethical fiber would be willing to make the supreme sacrifice for the sake of society or humankind in general, or for another individual, for a just and righteous cause.

MEIYO (TO) YUKI ✦ Honor and Courage

The word "honor" may be defined as a fine sense of what is just and right with readiness to apply it to one's own conduct in relation to others. Courage is the spirit that enables one to convert the willingness to apply righteousness and justice into deeds.

These two principles work hand in hand toward guiding and enforcing ones beliefs and views in life. Without honor, one will have little regard for oneself and may therefore act in a destructive fashion. If courage is lacking, honor is merely a noble thought with no substance. In such a case a person cannot be trusted to apply the lofty precepts of justice and righteousness to everyday life, especially if it becomes unpopular to do so.

The need to take physical action to champion the cause of right is a fact of history. Thomas Jefferson wrote that "The tree of liberty must be refreshed from time to time with the blood of patriots and tyrants." To shun such responsibilities after all other methods have been utilized, is submission rather than tranquility. In Shakespeare's *Hamlet,* Polonius advised his son, Laertes, "Beware of entrance to quarrel but being in/bear't that the opposed may beware of thee." This spirit is mandatory to *Budo.*

One aspect of life that influences human action in both positive and negative ways is the emotion of fear. Specifically, the fear of death. Since death is inevitable, life seems that much more precious and should be used wisely. But to allow fear to restrain you from acting in behalf of humanity is an improper course to chart.

The Japanese word *Daiojo* may be translated as "A peaceful death." This means that by living a constructive life and by practicing honor and courage we may meet death in a tranquil state regardless of the circumstances. This is an attitude which should be applied in conjunction with wisdom and correct judgment, in word as well as deed. The Japanese phrase *Bushi No Ichi Gon* ("The word of the warrior") conveys the attitude of taking pride in oneself and in having a sense of responsibility that leads away from acts of an unscrupulous nature. Honor and courage are the spine of the *Budo* precepts.

KOKKI ✦ Self-Conquest

The principle of *Kokki* teaches that a major focus of the *Budo* is self-improvement through continuous training. By winning over oneself we become better able to win over all adversities, including an opponent. In *The Art of War,* written by a mysterious Chinese warrior/philosopher named Sun-Tsu over two thousand years ago, it is stated "If we know the enemy and ourselves, there is no peril in a hundred battles. If we know not the enemy but know ourselves the odds are equal. If we are ignorant of both the enemy and ourselves, there is peril in a hundred battles."

Self-conquest leads to self-knowledge, which in turn leads to a greater knowledge of others. Winning and losing should be considered a learning experience and used as a tool for growth. Success is a by-product of effort in the *Budo;* therefore the journey becomes more important than the destination. Through self-conquest we may overcome negative aspects of our character, establish positive priorities, and obtain a greater prosperity in all aspects of our lives.

CHUJITSU ➤ Loyalty

According to *The American Heritage Dictionary of the English Language,* the word "loyalty" is defined as: "Faithful to a person, an ideal, a custom, a cause or a duty." It may be stated that loyalty is a cornerstone (along with honor and respect) of the *Budo* philosophy. In virtually all societies around the globe loyalty is considered an admirable quality. Loyalty is the foundation of trust, which plays a great role in human relationships. Loyalty is based on mutual caring, respect, and a sense of obligation toward those who extend aid and kindness in a sincere fashion. In the *Budo* it is considered inappropriate to leave the side of one with whom you have built a bond, due to popular societal opinion, self-gain, or fear. An oft-used example of loyalty is found in *The Tale of the 47 Ronin* (known as *Shijushichi Gishi* or *Chushingura* in Japanese). This is based on a true story that took place in Japan in 1701 A.D. A certain Lord Asano disrespected the dishonorable actions of a corrupt official of the Shogun's court in the capital of Edo (now Tokyo). Lord Asano drew his sword in anger in the confines of the palace, which was forbidden, and as a result was required to commit *Seppuku* (ritual suicide). Forty-seven of Lord Asano's loyal Samurai retainers vowed to exact vengeance on those responsible for their master's death. Through great self-sacrifice over a long period of time they eventually fulfilled their vow and in so doing relinquished their lives.

There was no hope of gain in their actions. Simply a duty of loyalty that at all costs had to be done. The tale of these brave stalwarts is legend and extols the virtue of loyalty.

BASIC PRINCIPLES AND AXIOMS OF BUDO

The following are basic principles and/or axioms that relate to the philosophy of the *Budo.* The underlying goal of all is self-improvement and self-development.

NINTAI / GAMAN　◆　Perseverance

Nintai and *Gaman* are two Japanese words with the same definition. Perseverance, endurance, and patience. Both *Nintai* and *Gaman* are commonly used in the martial arts and ways, and their shared meaning is highly regarded.

A "never say die" attitude is paramount to optimal success in the Budo. The race is not always to the swiftest but often to the surest. This thought is expressed in the fable of "the tortoise and the hare." *Kokoro Nintai* is a phrase meaning "the mind (heart or spirit) that perseveres." This should never be forgotten.

➤ See also "Nana Korobi Ya Okii"

SHU HA RI　◆　Obedience, Divergence, Separation

The principle of *Shu Ha Ri* (also called *Bun Shi Shu* or *Mamoru, Zabureru,* and *Janareru*) may be loosely translated as obedience, divergence, and separation, or transcendence. During the *Shu* stage the practitioner follows instructions exactly as transmitted by the teacher, thus developing correct basic form in the execution of technique. *Ha* indicates the stage whereby the practitioner, after arduously training to execute the techniques in the exact fashion prescribed, applies said techniques in a way that best fits his/her abilities and physical makeup. *Ri* is the phase where the practitioner becomes completely spontaneous, independent of preconception. Techniques become a natural reflex. This concept may be considered a circle.

No Form—natural instinct. In the beginning one does combatively what comes naturally.

Form—logical trained response. With training one follows the basic rules of combat that are more logically consistent with combative success.

Formless Form—through continuous training one finally returns to a phase of natural response and action, but this time with the aid of finely tuned technical skills, i.e., natural instinct blended with technique to form reflex action. This principle may be related not only to technique but to thought and philosophy as well.

In summary: *Shu Ha Ri*—to follow and maintain the tradition. To personalize the tradition. To transcend the tradition while maintaining the tradition.

BUNBU-RYODO — The Way of Both Academics and Martial Arts

This important concept in the *Budo* connotes the way of balanced, harmonious cultivation of the mind and body. The pursuit of excellence in all matters, civilian and military, as a united road toward continuous self-improvement.

The phrase *Bun Bu Ichi* is often translated as "the sword and the pen are one" and implies the importance of striving to become both a warrior and scholar in order to achieve a well rounded life. An exemplary character, strong spirit, and sound mind in a sound body. To be aware of the fact that all elements of one's existence should be developed is the essence of *Bunbu Ryodo*.

ORIME TADASHII — Correctly Creased

Orime Tadashii is a phrase that propounds the idea of presenting oneself properly in both appearance and conduct, both in and out of the Dojo. "Be careful with your thoughts because they can become words. Be careful with your words because they can become actions. Be careful with your actions because they can become habits. Be careful with your habits because they can become your character. Be careful with your character because it becomes your life."

UWATE NI WA UWATE ARI — Every Superior Has A Superior

The *Budo* teaches that there is no ultimate. There are always superior ideas and theories, but this principle is subject to change. At a given moment anyone can be bested. Examples of this may be seen throughout history. If we become entangled with being the best as opposed to simply being the best that we can be, we hinder our growth as human beings. Such an attitude leads to jealousy and other self-destructive thoughts. It leads to negative energy, self-doubt and insecurity.

Never live vicariously through the abilities and achievements of others. Emulate those with superior skills, but do so in the spirit of self-improvement. Skill and life are like the tide that flows and ebbs. There are always discussions about who or what is/was better between past and present. This does not matter. It has been stated that "Young Masters are respected, while old Masters are revered." Who is and/or was better is unimportant.

TORI WA ICHIJI NO HAJI, TOWANU WA MATSUDAI NO HAJI ➤

To Ask May Be A Moment's Shame, But Not To Ask And Remain Ignorant Is A Lifelong Shame

This adage means that we should never be to proud to seek knowledge. We should never be so concerned with ego and self-aggrandizement that we forget the quest for continuous improvement. If you don't know what lies on the road ahead, ask one who has traveled it.

ENRYO ➤ Reticence

Reticence may be defined as "being reserved." *Enryo* is a Japanese word that describes the attitude of not showing one's emotions. This is an integral aspect in the philosophy of the *Budo*. The ability to refrain from betraying emotions should be considered an admirable quality. The true warrior is compassionate and has deep and sincere feelings. However, these feelings are not shown to others at inappropriate times.

This attitude has historically been very important in combat. To show fear, pain, joy, or sorrow (in victory or defeat) could be fatal. *Enryo* may be related to an earlier philosophy that expressed the idea of "showing nothing." The Greek philosopher Zeno was a philosophical descendant of Socrates who, in about 300 B.C., organized a school of thought known as Stoicism, which was synonymous with inflexible self-control and rigorous living. The phrase *Bushi Wa Kuwaneido Taka Yoji* ("Although the warrior has not eaten, he uses his toothpick") epitomizes the concept of *Enryo*.

SATSUJINKEN / KATSUJINKEN ➤ The Sword That Takes Life / The Sword That Gives Life

This phrase may be used as a comparison of the Japanese martial arts *(Bugei* or *Bujutsu)* and the martial ways *(Budo)*. *Satsujinken* (the sword that takes life) expresses the goal of the ancient martial arts: to be as efficient and expedient as possible in defeating, i.e., killing, the opponent. *Katsujinken,* on the other hand, expresses one of the earliest cornerstones of the martial ways. To use the skills one develops through continuous training as a road to self-improvement throughout life.

The *Budo* came into being subsequent to the *Bugei,* as a result of the warriors' search for a deeper moral and spiritual base. It must be remembered, however, that the life and death practicality and seriousness in one's training must remain the same, even though the ultimate goal has changed.

NANA KOROBI YA OKII ➡ Seven Times Down, Eight Times Up

This maxim is well known in the *Bugei* and *Budo* and expresses the attitude of never giving up. In attempting to overcome bad habits or deleterious actions, "never quit quitting." In an effort to "be the best you can be," never stop trying. We all fall short at times of living up to our full potential. We all make mistakes. We are all subject to certain human frailties. "The largest room is the room for improvement." Even the best of us fail from time to time. We all have flaws. The Japanese saying *Saru Mo Ki Kara Ochiru,* ("Even monkeys fall out of trees") expresses this thought. This saying should not be used as a crutch to fail, but rather as a realization that we all in some way, at sometime, fall down, and we must pick ourselves up again. "Tough times don't last, tough people do."

GIRI ➡ Obligation Or Duty / Right Reason

Obligation or duty is highly regarded in the martial entities. It is based on the following system:

On—Favor
Giri—Obligation/Duty
Gimu—An unrepayable or life-long obligation

This system is prevalent in general Japanese society. To do a favor *(On)* for another creates *Giri* (obligation). A *Gimu* is considered a debt which cannot be repaid. An unending duty to those (family, friends, teachers, etc.) who give unconditional love, support, guidance, and assistance and with whom one has a strong bond *(Kizuna).* A feudal era form of *Giri* is termed *Adauchi* (an obligation of revenge). An example of this is found in the *Tale of the 47 Ronin.* In the *Budo Giri* is shown to those who, by their conduct and treatment of others, are deserving. *Giri* is a moral obligation based on what is right and just. It should be noted that included in this system is the word *Ninjo* (humanity/human feelings). This word is used to illustrate the contrast between what you want to do *(Ninjo)* and what you must do *(Giri).*

SHUGYO ➡ Austerity

In the English language austerity may be defined as the practice of severe discipline. The Japanese connotation of this word implies the strict discipline that is demanded in the pursuit of truth and enlightenment. This pertains to the rigorous training associated with the study of the martial arts.

The German philosopher Freidrich Nietzsche (1844–1900) wrote "That which does not kill me makes me stronger," and "Within every man lies a superman."

SABI SHIORI ➤ "Solitary Aloneness"

This term is found in Japanese aesthetics and may be related to the *Budo* in that it expresses a state of spirit whereby one subjects oneself to intense training, which is often of a solitary nature. An individual effort toward self-improvement. A desire and willingness to go beyond the regular efforts of the group.

FUDOSHIN ➤ Immovable Mind

This refers to an unshakable will or spirit that cannot be swayed or deterred from its goal. To focus all one's energies on a single point or purpose. To be unswerving in one's moral convictions and principles. Total concentration.

DO MU KYOKU ➤ "Life Beyond Limitation / To Train Throughout Life"

This adage expresses the concept that the martial way *(Budo)* is a lifetime journey, and training, a daily part of existence. This axiom encourages us to continue our pursuit of the way *(Do)* in spite of any physical limitations which we may incur due to age or injury. Improvement of mind and spirit may continue long after physical limits have been reached and it is for these reason that the true master is one who continues to train throughout a lifetime even though he/she may be long past prime or peak physical performance.

ZENSHO

Zensho is a term that relates to living each moment to the fullest and to being prepared to die without reservation. To live a complete life and die free of regret. This principle was, and is highly regarded by practitioners of the martial arts and ways. It conveys the reality that life is fleeting, and that it is therefore imperative to seize each moment and use it in a positive and productive fashion to its best advantage. By doing so one is better prepared to face the inevitable: death.

The Japanese Samurai were well aware of the fact that life was a day-to-day, even moment-to-moment proposition, since they faced the prospect of death constantly. By cultivating the principle of *Zensho* the *Bushi* (warriors) were better able to deal with the naturally inherent fear of death, thus freeing themselves to act without hesitation. In this way the Samurai developed an attitude that each day was a good day to die. Everyone dies, but not everyone truly lives.

The high regard in which the *Zensho* principle was held by the Samurai class may be seen in the fact that the famous Japanese swordsman Yamaoka Tesshu (1836–1888) named a temple (Zensho-An) that he founded after it. The principle of

Zensho is often related to the existence of the cherry blossom *(Sakura),* which suddenly blooms into an exquisite flower and just as quickly falls to the ground, thus fulfilling its role in nature. The Chinese Philosopher Lao Tse wrote "An inch of time is worth a foot of jade."

KYOBOKU KAZEYOSHI ➤ "Tall Trees Provoke The Pride Of Winds"

This maxim may also be translated as "the taller the tree, the stronger the wind that blows against it." This refers to the idea that within the bounds of human nature exists the emotion of envy. There will always be those that will denigrate the efforts and achievements of others, either due to envy or simply to raise their own station. It has been previously stated that "The mountain does not laugh at the river because it is lowly, nor does the river speak ill of the mountain because it cannot move about." This is a good axiom to express the idea of respect; however, it should be kept in mind that some rivers are polluted, and some mountains easily crumble. There are many roads to the mountain of enlightenment, but the wrong road leads nowhere.

"Action speaks louder than words." "Do unto others as you would have others do unto you." Train hard and consistently toward self-improvement. Be honest in your evaluation of yourself and others. Don't let ego overcome the quest for continuous knowledge and self-betterment. Take responsibility for your actions. In this fashion we may truly become tall trees.

THE MIDDLE COURSE

As previously mentioned, the word *Do* in *Budo* may be translated as "a course one follows or takes in life." The philosophy of *Budo* embraces what may be termed the "middle course." This is a positive and constructive attitude that aids the individual in seeking the essence of things and in exercising correct judgement.

The middle course avoids extremes and propagates a basic goodness that must become unshakable. Confucius wrote, "How transcendent is the moral power of the Middle Use! That it is but rarely found among the common people is a fact long admitted." People are too often influenced by emotions rather than practicality, and their thoughts and ideals may become contaminated by their surroundings and the state of the society. This may tend to lead one to follow a course that is harmful or destructive rather than one that is conducive to improvement of the individual and life in general. For these reasons we must become detached from our surroundings while being constantly aware. We must be able to react to all situations flexibly.

The *Budo-Ka* must become as adaptable as water, which shapes itself to all vessels that contain it. This type of adaptability is known in Japanese as *Rinkiohen,* and it is an important element of *Budo.* A noted Chinese philosopher of the Ming Dynasty stated that "If the mind be kept one and undivided it will accommodate itself to ten thousand varied circumstances. That is the reason why a superior man can keep his mind empty and undisturbed."

This type of unity in thought is necessary to keep from straying off the middle course. A sincere attempt must be made to follow the middle course at all times. Confucius stated that "Wealth and rank are what every man desires; but if they can only be retained to the detriment of the way he professes, he must relinquish them. Poverty and obscurity are what every man detests, but if they can only be avoided to the detriment of the way he professes, he must accept them. The gentleman who ever parts company with goodness does not fulfill that name. Never for a moment does a gentleman quit the way of goodness. He is never so harried but that he cleaves to this, never so tottering but that he cleaves to this."

Continuing with the merit of the middle course, another famous Chinese philosopher, Meng Tse (Moshi in Japanese and Mencius in Western society), said, "Benevolence is the heart of man; righteousness is the path of man. How lamentable a thing is it to leave the path and go astray, to cast away the heart and not know where to seek for it!"

The philosophy of *Budo* is complex in its simplicity. However, it may be said that *Budo* expresses what is termed in Japanese as *Seigi Jindo* (peace and humanity). To realize a happy, healthy, and rewarding existence through self-examination and self-improvement is the fundamental concept of *Budo.*

Budo is the working philosophy where thought and action are linked together to affect all areas of life. As human beings we must be responsible for our own cultivation before we can hope to raise the level of life on the whole. We cannot for example, ask our neighbors to keep their houses in order if our own home is in disarray. Martial entities such as *Karate-Do, Judo, Kendo, Aikido,* etc., are the vehicles of Budo and are inseparable from its goals and ideals. *Budo* is of great value to humanity and through dedication, patience, and determination the future of life collectively as well as individually may be greatly furthered and enhanced.

In conclusion, an appropriate thought was expounded by Confucius when he said "In the presence of a good man, think all the time how you may learn to equal him. In the presence of a bad man, turn your gaze within." Theories, philosophies, ideologies, and theologies may be corrupted, and it is for this reason that logical evaluation and adherence to the middle course must be followed.

THE SOCIETAL & HUMANITARIAN VALUE OF THE BUDO

There are three major elements that make up and influence life in general. These elements are the state of society, the state of nature, and the state of the individual. Each element (either directly or indirectly) has some effect on each other and are therefore somehow related.

THE STATE OF SOCIETY

As part of the world community, we must be aware of certain basic components that play a role in our existence. In a civilized society there are actions which are considered acceptable and those which are not. Opinions on what is morally and/or legally correct are usually determined by the beliefs of the general population of a given society. It is for this reason that the state of society in which we live directly affects our actions each day of our lives. Throughout history there are examples of societies that were morally and/or politically corrupt. These societies for the most part have perished, leaving little of value for the future of humanity. This is why it is of vital importance for each society in the world to have constructive ideas, principles, and life philosophies to guide their policies. The attitude of society can make

the difference between happiness or sadness, war or peace, intelligence or ignorance, health or illness, affluence or poverty, etc. The Budo serves as an example of
a positive, constructive lifestyle that propagates health, happiness, peace, and prosperity while taking into consideration the feelings and needs of humanity. The Budo
teaches harmony and justice with, and for, all human beings. If there were more
positive examples for society, it would help change the world for the better.

THE STATE OF NATURE

The state of nature plays an important role in life: the food we consume, the water
we drink, the air we breath. Even the weather that we experience each day greatly
affects our physical and mental well-being. In fact we may say that our natural surroundings have a bearing on all living things, both present and future. Each day we
hear of and see the way nature is abused by individuals and by society as a whole.
Misuse of chemicals and various forms of energy have caused great damage to the
land, sea, and air. It is often done for profit or power. This fact should be of concern
to all people of the world. If mankind is going to survive, we must learn to respect
and preserve nature. We must live in harmony with nature and all things. For these
reasons the Budo is important because it teaches respect and harmony in all things
at all times. It teaches growth toward the future. These principles, when applied to
the way we treat nature, can be a giant step toward improving our environment so
that the world will be a better place to live.

THE STATE OF THE INDIVIDUAL

In life each individual should be responsible for their actions. We must realize that
everything we do or say in some way, no matter how small, affects someone or
something else in life. The study of the *Budo* teaches us to know ourselves better. It
instills discipline and confidence in our lives, which makes us more productive
human beings. By gaining a positive individuality we may serve as a correct example to others. This has beneficial effects on life in general. Through the *Budo* we
may become healthy and happy because we gain an inner peace and a good and
moral character.

SUMMARY

Not all human beings have the ability or opportunity to change life on a world level, but each of us can make a contribution to the quality of life in one way or another. Through the *Budo* we may gain a strong mind and body and a good character. By our study of the *Budo* we become more aware of others and shun selfish attitudes. We strive to improve our knowledge and our ability and become more versatile by practicing the *Budo.*

It may be stated that the *Budo* is truly of unique value to society and humanity, and with the proper spread of the Budo it will be a positive influence for generations to come.

6

THE DOJO

BACKGROUND

"Dojo" is the Japanese pronunciation of the ancient Chinese word *Tao-Chang* (pronounced "Dao-Chang"). It comprises two Chinese characters. *Do*—way and *Jo*—place. In early China the Dojo was a place where astrologers, holy men, and mystics would interpret the "Way of the Heavens" and advise the emperor, who would in turn decide affairs of state accordingly.

During the eighth century A.D., it is believed that an esoteric monk named En-No-Gyoja traveled from China to the mountains of Japan, where he founded a group known as *Yamabushi* (mountain warriors). The *Yamabushi* practiced an eclectic form of Buddhism and mysticism and were said to have developed superhuman powers through breathing exercises, fasting, meditation, and severe physical training. Their practice was conducted in secret in caves and other natural settings called Dojo. On the island of Okinawa (and throughout the Ryukyu Island chain) there were special outdoor places of worship in most villages called *Umui.* These areas were usually located on a hilltop. Within the confines of the *Umui* was a clearing known as a *Miya.* It was in this area that Karate training was often conducted and may therefore be considered an early, natural Dojo. In a classical Japanese framework, the Dojo is a place where one learns and follows the way of a sacred ritual or traditional art or craft, in this case the martial arts. It is more than merely a school or gymnasium. It is a hallowed place where, for some, an entire way of life is cultivated. It is a place where not only physical skill, but more important, character, is highly developed; where moral and ethical precepts along with combat-related techniques and academics are transmitted, practiced, and absorbed. In the Dojo respect is earned and courtesy is demanded. Everyone starts at the bottom and everyone works. In this atmosphere a strong bond *(Kizuna)* is fostered between practitioners, which often spans a lifetime.

The Dojo often becomes a home away from home and in some cases home itself.

TYPES OF DOJO

There are several types of Dojo worthy of brief mention.

Bunko Dojo—branch school

Daigaku (University) Dojo—usually located in an appropriate area on campus. Generally speaking, this type of Dojo is often more of a club, primarily concerned with the sportive aspects of a martial discipline.

Honbu or *Hombu* Dojo—headquarters

Machi (Street) Dojo—This is the most common type of Dojo and is frequently a storefront, warehouse, or other commercial property.

Juku—This is a private school, sometimes a boarding school, usually concerned with instructing a small, select group. In times past the *Juku* was often associated with instruction in the Chinese classics (literature).

Kyoshitsu—This connotes a small room where instruction is often given on a one on one basis. In Japan a Dojo was often the teacher's garden or courtyard. It may be a park, a field, a beach, a basement, a garage, or (in the realm of my own experience) even an alley. Anywhere that training is conducted with sincerity *(Seijin)* may be considered a Dojo. In Zen thought the phrase "the world is your Dojo" aptly expressed this point.

PHYSICAL CHARACTERISTICS OF THE DOJO

Volumes could be written on the various physical characteristics of a traditional Dojo. The layout of the Dojo is determined by the practices, precepts, and ceremonies of a given martial discipline and also by the personal philosophy of the Dojocho (head of the Dojo). There are, however, certain basic principles that are observed universally in setting up a traditional Dojo. The training area is illustrated in diagram A. The *Shomen,* or main wall, is the focal point of the Dojo, a place where respect is shown to the concept of the Dojo. It is common to see a picture or photograph of the founder or patriarch of a system hanging in an appropriate place on the *Shomen.* This place may take the form of a recessed section or alcove in the wall, known as a *Tokonoma.* This area may be decorated with such articles as a *Shimenawa* (section of thick rope), *Gohei* (zig-zag strips of paper), *Katana* (Japanese sword), *Taiko* (drum), *Kakemono* (hanging scroll), *Bonsai* (miniature tree), or *Ikebana* (flower) arrangement. All of which further designate the *Shomen* as a place of honor. It should be noted that in some Dojo a *Shinza, Butsuden,* or *Kamidana* (types of shrines) may be found either in a *Tokonoma* or on a shelf attached to the *Shomen.*

This is not usually a religious shrine but rather symbolic of a place of deep respect. In some Dojo a type of Peg-Board which contain wooden tablets with the names of the Black Belt members *(Yudansha)* of said Dojo, may be displayed in an appropriate place. This is termed *Nafudakake.*

The surface of the training area is usually polished wood or *Tatami* (Japanese mats three-by-six feet made of rice straw *Toko* and covered with vinyl). In constructing a traditional-style Dojo, natural materials are often, used such as unfinished, unpainted wood. This conveys the Japanese concept of *Wabi* and *Sabi* (naturalness and rusticity). Japanese-style *Shojii* screens and sliding doors may also be found. An office *(Jimusho)* and changing area *(Kigaejo)* are commonly included sections of the *Dojo.* In all areas a clean, simple, neat and natural atmosphere is strived for.

DIAGRAM OF THE DOJO (TRAINING AREA)

SHOMEN (Main Wall)

JOZA OR KAMIZA
(Upper Seat)

SHIMOSEKI
(Lower Side)

KEIKOBA (Practice Area)
TAIJO (Body Place)
or
RENSHUJO (Training Place)

JOSEKI
(Upper Side)

SHIMOZA
(Lower Seat)

THE SPIRIT OF THE DOJO

A good Dojo develops and exudes its own character. This is a special feeling or spirit referred to as *Kami*. It is the soul of the Dojo. In the Japanese martial arts and ways a place like a Dojo or an object like a sword is believed to express a certain spirit. This should not be confused with the type of spirit *(Seishin)* that is developed by people, such as a team or class spirit. A good Dojo spirit is important in the correct transmission of all aspects of *Karate-do*. The development of Dojo spirit is based on austerity *(Shugyo)*, sincerity *(Seijin)*, and effort *(Kunren)*. Observance of proper etiquette and ceremony is integral in creating an atmosphere that pushes pupils to reach their maximum potential.

A strong Dojo spirit precludes laziness. Upon entering, it becomes clear that this is a serious place, which prompts students to do their best.

HISTORICAL NOTES ON THE DOJO

NYUMON ➧ Entering the Gate

Joining a traditional Dojo was in times past termed "entering the gate." *(Nyumon)*. In common parlance, *Nyumon* may be considered "introduction," not in the sense of an introduction to another person but rather an introduction to a subject, path, or way *(Michi* or *Do)*.

In ancient times the size, shape, and type of gate or entrance *(mon)* to a Dojo designated the status of the teacher. It could be an ornate archway, (or even sacred, as in Shintoism) or simply a basic doorway. Unlike the modern practice of accepting anyone that walks in with money, the policy of traditional Dojo was one of discouraging entrance due to the severity of the "road" ahead. Only those that truly had the tenacity and patience to undergo any and all tests put to them were accepted as disciples *(Deshi)*. Letters of recommendation were often required to "Enter the Gate," and patience was tested by making the applicant come back over and over again before being allowed an audience with the teacher. In this fashion the sincerity and intent of the prospective pupil was determined. The sign *(Kamban)* of a traditional Dojo also had great significance. Some proclaimed simply the name of the *Ryu* or *Ryuha* (system or style), while others declared a challenge to those who thought of entering, such as *Shoko Kyakka* (watch out, or watch your step). This relates to an attitude of "Enter at your own risk!" In other words, this road is going to be very difficult, so beware! A sign that best expressed the idea of undertaking training at a traditional Dojo was the phrase *Kamawan*. This may be broken down as *Kama* (sickle) and *Wan* (rice bowl). In the colloquial Japanese usage this means "I dare you!" The characters for *Kamawan* were also used on the hand guards *(Tsuba)* of Japanese swords.

The basic criteria for entering a traditional martial discipline was love for the art, the courage to undergo the severe training, and reverence and devotion to the master or teacher.

DOJO YABURI / DOJO ARASHI ➤ Breaking the Dojo / Challenging the Sensei

This was an old custom of going to a Dojo and challenging the students and teacher to combat. *Dojo Yaburi* often took place as a result of one group being insulted by another; as a method of testing skill, as in the case of a *Mushashugyo* (a Samurai who travelled around refining technique through contest); or merely to prove superiority, thus gaining notoriety. This practice may be compared to the European custom of dueling. This custom is of course refrained from in modern times, as it is contrary to the *Budo* ethic.

REIGISAHO AND REISHIKI ➤ Etiquette And Ceremony

"Respect is earned, courtesy demanded." This expression aptly explains the attitude that should govern Dojo conduct.

In as much as *Karate-Do* is a military or martial discipline, it should come as no surprise that a well-structured code of etiquette and ceremony be followed in its practice. This preserves order, allows for greater concentration, eliminates wasted time, promotes discipline, and reduces unnecessary injuries from uncontrolled activity.

Proper procedure in this area produces an atmosphere where instruction may be given and received more readily.

REI ➤ Salutation or Bowing

In Japan, salutations are expressed by bowing and since *Karate-Do* is a Japanese martial tradition, it is important to be aware of certain basic methods of bowing that are most commonly used in training. There are two basic types of bowing: *Ritsurei* (standing bow) and *Zarei* (seated bow). The depth and duration of a bow is determined by ones stature or position in relation to another. In this regard bowing may be further divided into three categories:

Shin—used when saluting one of junior rank.
Gyo—used when saluting one of equal rank.
So—used when saluting one of senior rank.

A general rule is the higher the rank or status of the person you are bowing to, the lower and longer you bow. There are many times when bowing is required. The following are some of the most common: when entering and exiting the training area (done while facing the *Shomen)*; before and after practicing with a partner; to a senior before and after asking a question or receiving instruction; to the *Sensei* at the beginning and end of an encounter and at the opening and closing of class.

Some other terms related to bowing are *Keirei* (a very formal bow executed very slowly), *Reihai* (a deep bow of respect), *Gassho* (a bow done with the hands together in front of the face, palms touching/as in a prayer position), and *Han Gassho* (the same as *Gassho* but with only one hand).

SOJI ← Cleaning The Dojo

Cleaning the Dojo is a common practice in the traditional martial arts and ways. It serves the practical purpose of keeping the training hall neat and clean, but beyond this it develops a sense of pride in the Dojo among trainees as well as instilling an attitude of working together. *Soji* is generally done either before or after formal training sessions.

STRUCTURE OF SENIORITY IN THE DOJO

SENPAI (SEMPAI) / KOHAI / DOHAI

From the beginning of time in virtually all societies there has existed a caste system or structure of seniority. This is true even in the animal kingdom. It is important to have this type of defined structure of station or position to avoid chaos.

In the military this is known as the chain of command. This is also found in law enforcement. It is therefore no surprise that there is a well defined order of seniority in the traditional martial arts and ways of Japan. The Japanese observe a social structure simply termed *Tate Shakai,* or vertical society. This consists of a *Oyabun* (parent), *Kobun* (child), and the rights and responsibilities *(Mibun)* of each. The terms *Oyabun* and *Kobun* are used figuratively in that this system is applied to all areas of society and not just the family. This structure is more commonly known as the *Senpai/Kohai* (senior/junior) system.

In the martial arts and ways this structure is strictly adhered to not only inside the Dojo but outside as well. There is always mutual respect and consideration between *Senpai* and *Kohai.* Formalities in word and deed are observed according to rank and stature.

Basically, the *Senpai* has a responsibility to instruct, correct, and lead the *Kohai* properly in the study of the *Budo,* while the *Kohai* has the responsibility to receive and follow the instructions, corrections, and leadership of the *Senpai.*

Practitioners of equal rank and stature are termed *Dohai.*

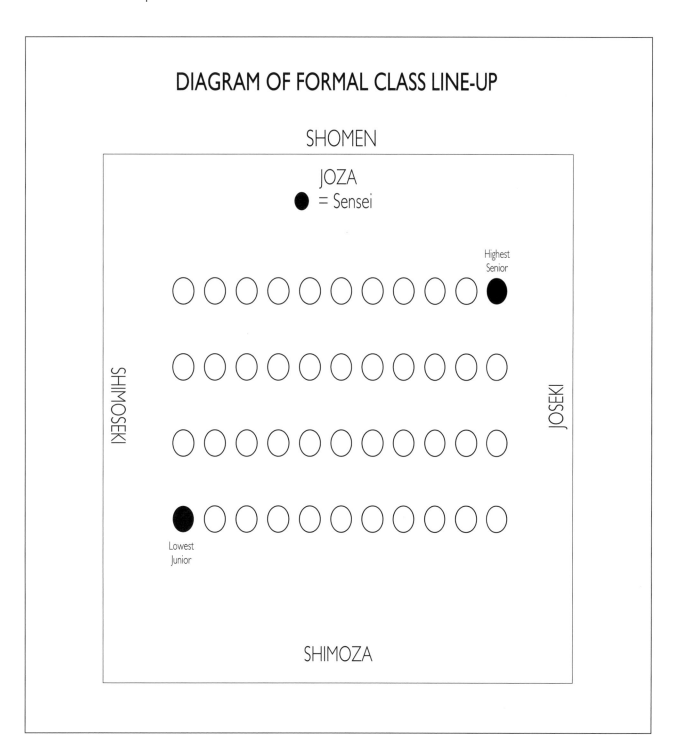

7

THE CLASS

SENSEI ← Teacher

The word *Sensei* may basically be defined as teacher. It may technically be described as "one born earlier" or "one who goes before." This term is often used in Japanese to denote a person of laudable character or status and wisdom, one who guides others on a prescribed path. In Karate, the *Sensei* is the signpost which points the direction on the journey toward self-improvement and enlightenment. The *Sensei* should be held in high esteem and is always treated with appropriate respect. The *Sensei* undertakes a grave and solemn responsibility and must be compassionate and strict, kind and harsh, forgiving and unrelenting in an attempt to show the way. The *Sensei* must follow a difficult course, one which often seems a dichotomy. The *Sensei* must be seemingly superhuman while still being a mere mortal. The *Sensei* must be many things to many people/a difficult task to say the least.

Karate is a martial discipline and as such it must be considered in a military structure. It is a benevolent dictatorship, where the word of the *Sensei* (in matters of training) is law. This method leads to discipline and focus of effort, which is conducive to achieving the goal of self-improvement. The *Sensei/Deshi* (master/disciple, teacher/pupil) relationship is sacred in Karate. It is a special bond built on mutual respect, trust and hard training, It has been said that "Young masters are respected, but old masters are revered."

KEIKOGI ← Practice Uniform

The practice uniform is known by various names in Japanese: *Renshugi* (training uniform), *Budogi* (martial way uniform), *Karategi* (empty hand uniform), *Dogi* (way uniform) and, most commonly, *Gi*. The practice uniform is made up of the jacket *(Uwagi)*, trousers *(Zubon)* and the belt *(Obi)*. The jacket was adopted from the *Hanten* (a quilted jacket worn by men during the feudal period). The collar is called

Eri and the sleeves, *Sode.* The string ties used to hold the jacket together are termed *Uwagi Jime.* The trousers were adopted at a latter stage.

Originally the lower garment used in the practice of Karate, Jujutsu, etc. was a *Fundoshi* (loincloth) or sometimes a *Hakama* (divided skirt).

Often a *Hachimaki* (headband) is worn in practice. The *Hachimaki* prevents hair and perspiration from getting in the eyes, and putting on the *Hachimaki* is symbolic of preparing for hard work, just as rolling up the sleeves is in Western culture.

FORMAL CLASS OPENING AND CLOSING PROCEDURE

HAKKAI SHIKI ➤ Opening Procedure

Kiosuke—Line up.
Seiza—Formal seated posture.
Mokuso—Meditation/Reflection.
Yame—To stop or end.
Sensei Ni Rei—Pupils and teacher bow to each other.
Otagai Ni Rei—Pupils bow to the teacher.
Kiritsu—Stand or rise.

TEUCHI SHIKI ➤ Closing Procedure

Same as *Hakkai Shiki.*

All commands are called by the senior pupil. When lining up, pupils move quickly to form straight, even rows according to and rank assume the *Musubi Dachi*—heels together with palms touching the sides of the thighs, back straight, eyes forward. Pupils assemble according to rank facing the teacher, with seniors to the left.

When students do *Otagai Ni Rei* at the beginning of class, they recite *"Onegai Shimasu."* This means "please do me a favor." The students are in effect asking the teacher to do them the favor or honor of instructing them. This is a sign of respect. The phrase *Onegai Shimasu* is also said by students to each other before practicing in pairs.

When students do *Otagai Ni Re* at the end of class, they recite *Domo Arigatto Gozaimashita,* which means "thank you very much." The students are thanking the instructor at this time for guiding them in their training. When students finish an exercise that requires a partner, they say simply *"Arigatto Gozaimashita."* In this way the students acknowledge the help they have given each other during the exercise. At the end of formal class, when the students and teacher stand, it is sometimes customary for them to bow to each other once again, at which time the teacher says, *"Go Kuro Sama Deshita,"* which means, "thank you for your trouble." In this way, the teacher is showing his or her respect for the students by thanking them for taking the time and trouble to practice with him or her and for being receptive to his or her teachings.

When one assumes the formal seated posture *(Seiza)*, the left knee touches the ground at the right heel, then the right knee touches the ground with the instep of the foot resting on the sole of the left foot. The back should be straight and there should be approximately six inches of space between the knees. The palms of the hand should be placed on the thighs with the fingertips pointing inward. When rising from the formal seated posture the right heel touches the ground at the left knee as you rise on the right leg, then the left. An alternate method is to kneel on both legs at the same time.

MOKUSO ← Reflection Or Meditation

Mokuso is done both before and after formal practice to relax the body and clear the mind. Sitting in *Seiza* (the formal seated posture), the eyes are closed and the neck is straight. Breathing should be done through the nose in a deep, slow fashion. The entire body should be completely relaxed. Before starting practice, the mind should be made a blank. This will allow freedom from outside thoughts, which can be distracting. A simple exercise which may be used to clear the mind is to concentrate on a single object (such as a lighted bulb) to the exclusion of all else. This will help the concentration and prepare one to focus total energy on training. After practice, the student should reflect upon the training that was just completed and attempt to relate to these studies on an individual basis.

TAISO ◆ Calisthenics

Calisthenics are an important part of Karate training. Prior to the start of physical Karate practice, preparatory calisthenics *(Jumbi Undo)* are done to loosen and stretch the muscles, joints, tendons, and ligaments. These exercises also increase the intake of oxygen and stimulate blood circulation. The heart and lungs are strengthened and do not become fatigued as easily during strenuous training. As the body is thoroughly warmed, mobility is gained and reflexes become more rapid. By performing preparatory calisthenics, the risk of injury (such as pulls, strains, sprains, and dislocations) during Karate practice is greatly reduced. Exercises should be done in a pattern, starting with lower extremities and working upward to promote circulation and to avoid putting too much stress on the heart too soon. This type of warming up also relaxes the mind and relieves tension so that better concentration can be achieved in training.

After practice, warm down calisthenics *(Seiri Undo)* should be performed to relax the body and to gradually cool down. The pulse and respiration rate is slowed to normal, and lactic acid is burned as more oxygen is carried to the muscles and circulation is improved. This process helps prevent the joints from stiffening and the muscles from cramping.

RENSHU/KEIKO — Training /Practice

The word *Renshu* may be defined as training and Keiko as practice. Training may be thought of as the instruction received, which is then studied and practiced *(Keiko)*. These terms are, however, commonly interchangeable. Renshu may be literally defined as "forging (or polishing) lessons," referring to hard, continuous work through repetition of the basics *(Kihon)* to sharpen technique, as opposed to merely learning new material. The word *Keiko* also implies a deeper significance. It is derived from the ancient Chinese and is found in Japan in the early text *Kojiki* ("The Record of Ancient Matters") as *Keiko Shokon* ("To learn from the past to understand the present"). *Keiko* has come to express an attitude of learning by doing, a spirit whereby one attains character development as well as physical cultivation, and ultimately understanding and enlightenment *(Satori)*, through mastery of one's chosen art by way of hard and constant effort, i.e., practice.

The following are classifications of training and practice:

Godoo Renshu—Group training.

Kojin Renshu—Individual training.

Kihon Renshu—Basic training.

Chukyu Renshu—Intermediate training.

Jokyu Renshu—Advanced training.

Dokuso Geiko—To practice by oneself.

Hikitate Geiko—Form of practice where a senior guides a junior.

Gishiki Barame Geiko—Informal or open practice where pupils can work on what they wish.

Gasshuku—Billeting. Special training and practice. This form of special training usually refers to a camp setting where most of the training takes place out-of-doors, close to nature

Shochugeiko—Special summer practice.

Kangeiko—Special winter practice. (Both *Shochugeiko* and *Kangeiko* are traditionally conducted in the *Gasshuku* format).

Kamoku—A clinic or seminar conducted by a guest instructor.

Koshu—A short class or course taught by an instructor of the same school.

Misogi—This is a form of special training, adapted from Shinto monks, that is a rite of purification through deprivation (e.g., without sleep, food, drink, etc.). In its original form it was often accompanied by chanting and the ringing of bells.

Kogangeiko—This is a form of special training whereby members of a different *Ryu* (school, style or system) get together to exchange ideas and techniques, often through *Kumite.*

OUTLINE OF KOEI-KAN KARATE-DO CURRICULUM ➤ Kyoka

PHYSICAL TRAINING ➤ Karada No Renshu

PART I. *TAISO* (CALISTHENICS)

A. *Jumbi Undo* (Preparatory or Warm-up exercises)

B. *Seiri Undo* (Warm-down exercises)

C. *Hojo Undo* (Auxiliary exercises)

   1. Cardiovascular exercises

   2. Strengthening exercises

   3. Reflex and Mobility exercises

PART II. *WAZA* (TECHNIQUES)

Natural Weapons

A. Foundational Techniques

   1. *Tachi Kata* and *Kamae* (Stances and Guards)

   2. *Tenshin Waza* or *Tenshinho* (Body Transfer/Dodging Techniques)

   3. *Kokyu Waza* or *Kokyuho* (Breathing Techniques)

B. Primary Techniques

   1. *Uke Waza* (Blocking Techniques)

   2. *Tsuki* or *Zuki Waza* (Punching Techniques)

   3. *Keri Waza* (Kicking Techniques)

   4. *Uchi* (or *Ate) Waza* (Striking Techniques)

C. Secondary Techniques

   1. *Nage No Kata* (Throwing Methods)

   2. *Shime Waza* (Choking Techniques)

   3. *Gyaku-Te* (Joint Reversal Techniques)

   4. *Hazushi Waza* (Escaping Techniques)

D. General Techniques

   1. *Tori* or *Toru Waza* (Grabbing or Holding Techniques)

   2. *Kyo Waza* (Faking or Feinting Techniques)

   3. *Suwari Waza* (Seated Techniques)

   4. *Newaza* (Techniques of Fighting on or from the Ground)

   5. *Osae Waza* (Pressing or Pining Techniques)

   6. *Renzoku* (or *Renraku) Waza* (Combination Techniques)

   7. *Shirahaderi* (Defense Against Bladed Weapons)

      A. *Tanto Bogyo* (Knife Defense) A.K.A. *Tanto Dori* (Knife Taking)

      B. *Tachi Bogyo* (Sword Defense) A.K.A. *Tachi Dori* (Sword Taking)

8. *Tateki Uchi* (Defense Against Multiple Attackers)
9. Defense Against an Attacker Armed with Non bladed Weapons
10. *Sasoi Waza* (Allurement Techniques—Leaving openings, etc.—To Draw the Opponent In)
11. *Katame Waza* (Close-Quarter Techniques, Which May Include Grappling, Pining, Choking, Joint Reversals, etc.)
12. *Goshinjutsu* (Specialized Techniques of Self-Defense)
13. *Kenju Bogyo* (Gun Defense)

NOTE: Foundational, Secondary, and General Techniques may be divided into defensive *(Bogyo)* and offensive *(Kogeki)*.

PART III. APPLICATIONS OF TECHNIQUES

A. *Kihon Renshu* (Basic Training)
   1. *Kihon Dai Ichi:* Basics No. 1 (Techniques done Singularly)
   2. *Kihon Dai Ni:* Basics No. 2 (Techniques Done in Pairs)
   3. *Kihon Dai San:* Basics No. 3 (Techniques Done in Combinations of Three or More)
B. *Kumite,** *Gumite* or *Sante* (Practice Matching or Sparring)
   1. *Ippon Gumite* (1 Point Matching)
   2. *Nihon Gumite* (2 Point Matching)
   3. *Sanbon Gumite* (3 Point Matching)
   4. Others: *Yohon, Gohon,* etc.
   5. *Renzoku Gumite* (Continuous Give-and-Take Matching)
   6. *Jiyu Kumite* (Free Matching—Various types)
   7. *Bogu Kumite* or *Bogu Shiai* (Free Matching with Protective Gear)

PART IV. *KATA* (FORM)

A. *Fukyu Kata* (Dissemination) *Kata:* Forms or Patterns Created to Transmit Basic Techniques in a Logical Sequence
B. *Koryu Kata* (Ancient or Classical/Traditional *Kata*)

***NOTE:** *Kumite* may be literally defined as *Kumi*—Grappling and *Te*—Hand.

ACADEMICS ◆ Gaku

I. History *(Reishiki)*

II. Philosophy *(Tetsugaku)*
(Budo)

III. Science *(Kagaku)*

    A. Anatomy *(Kaibogaku)*
    Study of:

        1. The Skeletal System

        2. The Muscular System

        3. The Nervous System

        4. The Sense Organs

        5. The Circulatory System

        6. The Respiratory System

        7. The Digestive System

        8. The Urinary System

    B. Attacking Vital Points *(Kyusho/Atemi)*

    C. Resuscitation / First Aid *(Katsu)*

    D. Chinese Medicine *(Kampo)*

    E. Massage and Manipulation

    F. Physics

    G. Kinetics

8

Tenshin Waza

Techniques of Body Transfer

Tenshin Waza is a key area of training in *Koei-Kan Karate-Do*. The body transfer techniques used in the *Koei-Kan* curriculum were developed by Master Onishi Eizo (the founder). Through his detailed and arduous studies he formulated a comprehensive system of body movement, much of which is unique to the *Koei-Kan* system in its categorization and application. Body movement, to one degree or another, may be found in virtually all martial entities, both past and present. The following verse taken from Chinese boxing illustrates the importance placed upon movement. "Edging and dodging need sharp eyesight; You must move fast to left and right/ To dodging, edging owes/ From the unreal the real goes/ A mountain slide you may escape/ by wedging ahead through the gape/ Flinch not at actions furious/ To beat the great with the small is truly curious."

Tenshin techniques are applied both defensively and offensively. They are used to dodge or evade, attack and counterattack an opponent or opponents. In the dodging *(Kawashi)* capacity, techniques of body transfer are imperative to combative effectiveness because one may be confronted by:

A. An opponent that is larger and physically more powerful.
B. Multiple attackers.
C. An armed attacker.
D. Multiple armed attackers.

Timing, speed, coordination and balance are the keys to effective *Tenshin*. There are fourteen basic *Tenshin* techniques used in *Koei-Kan*. From these essential methods countless variations and combinations may be derived. Each technique of body transfer should be first practiced singularly in all possible directions. Then they should be combined and varied and applied conjunctively with the blocking, striking, kicking, and punching techniques.

In an offensive mode, techniques of body transfer make it possible to transmit a maximum amount of body weight into an attack. It also enables one to use an opponent's force to one's own advantage. Defensively, techniques of body transfer make it possible to evade the attack and take full advantage of any openings thus created. Certain body transfer techniques are designed to cover a desired distance rapidly, to either close in on the opponent or put the opponent's attack out of range. Ability in *Tenshin Waza* enhances overall combative efficiency.

> **NOTE:** Techniques of falling and rolling *(Taore* and *Ten Waza,* respectively) are often grouped together under the general heading of *Taore Waza.* The term *Kawashi* (dodging) is specifically applied to techniques of body transfer used for evasive purposes.
>
> Another Japanese term (outside of Koei-Kan) commonly used to describe body movement is Tai Sabaki.

TENSHIN WAZA ➤ Body Transfer Techniques / Footwork

The following *Tenshin* Techniques are the most practical, and therefore the most useful, methods of body transfer. They are illustrated here in the form of footprint diagrams. The shaded footprints represent the start position. The numbers 1 and 2 represent the sequence in which the movement should be executed.

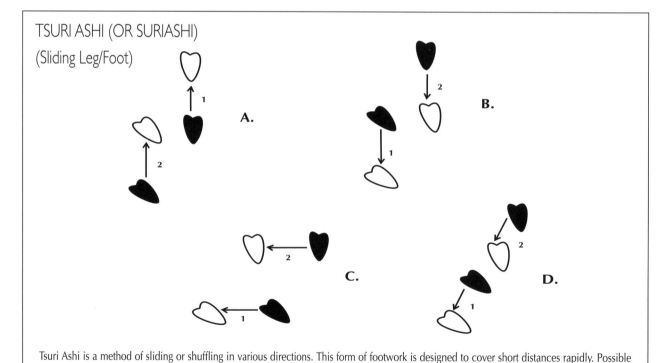

TSURI ASHI (OR SURIASHI)
(Sliding Leg/Foot)

A.

B.

C.

D.

Tsuri Ashi is a method of sliding or shuffling in various directions. This form of footwork is designed to cover short distances rapidly. Possible directions are forward (A), backward (B), sideways, left or right (C), and diagonally, forward or backward (D).

YOKO IDO
(Side Move or Step)

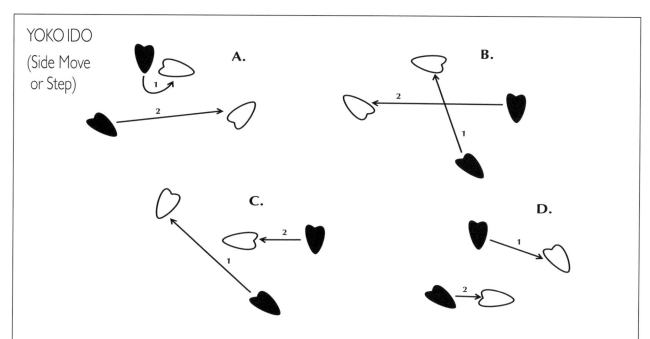

Yoko Ido is a method of footwork that may be applied when going to the inside (Uchi) or outside (Soto) of an opponent. It is most commonly used defensively to evade an attack. There are four basic methods which (for the purpose of classification) may be termed Dai Ichi (No. 1) as illustrated in diagram A, Dai Ni (No. 2) as illustrated in diagram B, Dai San (No. 3) as illustrated in diagram C, and Dai Yon (No. 4) as illustrated in diagram D.

EREKAE
(Leg Change)

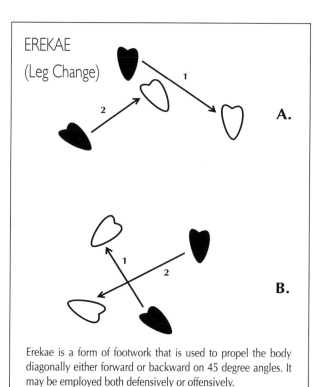

Erekae is a form of footwork that is used to propel the body diagonally either forward or backward on 45 degree angles. It may be employed both defensively or offensively.

MAWARI KOMI
(Circle Step)

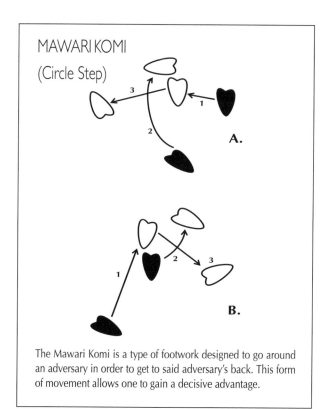

The Mawari Komi is a type of footwork designed to go around an adversary in order to get to said adversary's back. This form of movement allows one to gain a decisive advantage.

9

KATA

FORM

Within the structure of most systemized martial arts and ways, the practice of *Kata* is an integral aspect. Traditionally *Kata* have been used to transmit the syllabus/curriculum of a system from teacher to pupil, one generation to the next. It is intended to convey the underlying principles of technique rather than merely to teach specific combat responses to specific combative situations.

Kata serves the purpose of instilling certain fundamental skills that are prerequisite to the successful execution of a given art through a logical predetermined pattern, thus simplifying the memorization process of said skill. This type of practice drill is often seen in the military, e.g., the manual of arms, etc. *Kata* are often used as a part of a pupils criteria for grading.

The nearest English equivalent for the Japanese word *Kata* is the word "form": a set method or pattern of doing or practicing something. In Karate, *Kata* is considered a valuable and important area of training. *Kata* may be found in a wide variety of Japanese arts and crafts outside those of a martial or military nature, such as Japanese dance, theater, the tea ceremony, etc.

Basically, *Kata* may be defined as a combination of offensive and defensive techniques organized systematically into a continuous series of movements. It is designed to develop in the practitioner speed, timing, coordination, balance, correct execution and focus of techniques, proper breathing, precise eye contact, rapid body transfer, and quick reflexes. In addition to these benefits, regular *Kata* training aids in strengthening muscles and bones, increases stamina, and promotes overall good health.

Kata may be practiced almost anywhere, and no auxiliary equipment is necessary. For this reason, *Kata* is a very practical method of daily exercise. Within these formal prearranged patterns, the applications of various techniques in actual combat or self defense situations may be found. *Kata* was one of the original ways in which Karate was practiced and is, therefore, of historical importance. The older or more ancient *Kata* are known as *Koryu Kata*.

It is interesting to note that many Kata begin with defensive technique, thus expressing the saying *Karate Ni Sente Nashi* (there is no first attack in Karate). This important principle means that Karate is a defensive rather than offensive art and should not be used in an aggressive manner.

Some *Kata* are composed of simple or more basic techniques and movements, while others are very intricate and complex.

There are over fifty classical Okinawan *Kata.* The majority are of Chinese origin and have undergone revision on Okinawa and in Japan. The Okinawan Kata may be broken into either *Naha-Te, Shuri-Te* or *Tomari-Te.*

In the past, as many as three years were spent on just one Kata so that it could be executed as closely to perfection as possible and so that it could be totally understood. This attitude is expressed in the Japanese saying *Hito Kata San-Nen.* It would be wise to let this example show us the importance of constant and continual training in *Kata.*

AREAS OF PERFORMANCE

A. Since all Kata are composed of a predetermined sequential order of techniques, proper execution depends on a thorough observation of this order.

B. All Kata have a prescribed directional pattern, known as the *Embusen* or *Engisen* (line of performance). It is, therefore, important to be aware of all steps, lunges, pivots, lengths, and widths of stances, and all other body motions that may be required.

C. The word *Kime* (focus) refers to the application of techniques to specific target areas throughout the Kata and to the instant concentration of force and muscle contraction at the exact point of impact. This point is imperative in obtaining the power that a strong *Kata* demands. It is this principle which is most responsible for giving *Kata* a crisp, sharp appearance.

D. Each *Kata* has a certain pace or rhythm to which it should be performed, and care should be given to pauses that may occur between movements.

Timing is one of the major factors in the performance of Kata. There is usually a pause after the execution of technique. This pause may be termed *Zanshin* (remaining spirit), which expresses continuous concentration and alertness. It is said that "The dead tiger kills the most hunters." For this reason the principle of Zanshin is important to the martial arts and ways.

All motions should be fluid and flexible and should blend with the desired rhythm. In stepping, lunging and pivoting, the hips should move along a smooth, even plane without rising and falling in a choppy fashion. Each change in stance should flow one into the next. Motions should never be jerky.

E. Force should be manifested through the proper use of hips *(Koshi)* and the lower abdominal region *(Tanden)* in conjunction with the motions of the extremities.

F. Complete balance must be maintained at all times. Any lack of stability during the performance of *Kata* will greatly decrease effectiveness.

G. Proper eye contact *(Metsuke)* is necessary to the practice of *Kata*. The term "eye contact" denotes the focal point where vision is directed during execution. This point is usually on a level equal to that of the performer's own eyes, although this point may change from time to time. The eyes should be in their natural state of openness, and undue squinting or blinking should be avoided. The eyes should be focused rapidly to the appropriate spot in conjunction with each change in direction.

H. Proper formation of the various techniques are imperative. Placing the hands and feet in the correct position influences the meaning of the application. Moreover, the point from which the technique originates and the form of the required motion must be constantly considered.

I. Correct breathing *(Kokyu)* is integral in the performance of *Kata*. Generally, inhalation occurs prior to the execution of a technique or movement, and exhalation is done at the exact moment of delivery. During periods of respiration, the body is relaxed, while at times of expiration, the body is slightly tensed. Inhaling and exhaling aids in expanding and contracting the muscles, thus assisting body relaxation and tension.

Generally, breathing in *Kata* is soundless; however, some *Kata* employ methods of breathing that are very deep and forceful and are easily audible. An important aspect directly related to breathing that is utilized in many *Kata* is the *Kiai*.

Basically, the *Kiai* may be defined as "superpower" or "spirit-letting." It is the yell or scream so often heard in relation to Karate. The *Kiai* serves three major purposes. First it helps to psychologically unnerve the opposition. Second it bolsters one's own courage. Finally, the *Kiai* assists in releasing adrenaline into the blood stream, thus adding power to an attack. The *Kiai* is done by exhaling sharply through the mouth in the form of a short yell. The breath should be brought up from the diaphragm, and the abdomen should be tensed instantly. In *Kata* there will usually be one or two specific points where *Kiai* is required.

J. *Kata* demands the performer's utmost concentration. This type of concentration is known technically as *Fudoshin* (the immovable mind). In effect this means that one's mind is totally fixed to the Kata being executed. Through constant practice over a very long period, a state called *Mushin* (the nothing mind) will be achieved. At this point, the mind is completely attuned to every movement and is free of all thought, so that a unity of mind and body is accomplished. At this stage Kata will be natural, and all motions will be reflex action.

K. Each movement of the *Kata* has a meaning and should be analyzed and thoroughly understood. Some techniques often may be applied in a variety of ways in connection with actual combat. The application of *Kata* technique is called *Bunkai.* When executing *Kata,* the value of the combative applications should be kept in mind, and each motion must be done in earnest, as if the practitioner were applying them in a real situation. This attitude may be termed *(Tokon)* fighting spirit, and it is this aspect which gives the *Kata* a dynamic and realistic appearance while greatly enhancing its purpose. There are often combative applications that are not readily seen. These are known as *Kakushi* or *Kakushite* (hidden or hidden hand), and were included in the *Kata* by the developing Masters to disguise the more dangerous techniques. In this regard there is a similarity between Okinawan Karate *Kata* and the traditional royal Okinawan dance called *Ukansen Odori.* There are Okinawan dance techniques termed *Ogamite* (praying hands), *Konerite* (twisting hands), *Osute* (pushing hands), etc. These are called *Meikata,* and these techniques may very well have been integrated to one degree or another into the Karate *Kata* in order to give an innocuous appearance to the more lethal techniques. In this fashion the *Sensei* would be able to pick and choose those who were felt to be of a stellar character and who would refrain from using said lethal tactics indiscriminately.

L. *Kata* begins and ends with the traditional *Ritsu-Rei* (standing salutation). This is an expression of humility and sincerity, which is representative of the Karate spirit.

In summation, the Japanese principle *Kata No San Yoso* (which pertains to the three most important areas of Kata performance) should be kept in mind. These areas are the correct application of force at the proper time *(Chikara No Kiyo-Zaki),* correct body movement and execution of technique with proper form *(Karada No Shin-Shiku),* and correct rhythm, speed, and timing *(Wada No Dan Kyu).*

KATACHI ➤ The Soul of Kata

Katachi may be considered the soul of *Kata*. It is the aura or energy generated by the execution of a truly superb *Kata*. It is an acute feeling of focusing the mind, body, and spirit on each motion while embracing the reality of the application. *Katachi* expresses the inner or hidden teachings *(Okuden)* within *Kata*. The characters that comprise the word *Katachi* may be broken down as follows: *Ka,* from the word *Kami* or *Kamisama* (God/Supreme Being); *Ta,* indicating a field (for crops); and *Chi,* indicating a type of energy or power found in words such as *Mizuchi* (the deities of water) and *Ikazuchi* (the deities of lightning) from Japanese folklore. The combination of these three characters may suggest man's basic nature, roots, existence, and working/cultivating (the soil, or *Ta)*; man's striving to reach a higher, loftier plane *(Ka)*; and the energy/power required to accomplish this task *(Chi)*. This conveys the deeper, more esoteric elements of *Kata*.

"When you do *Kata* a thousand times you begin to understand the application. When you do Kata five thousand times you begin to see your opponents. When you do Kata ten thousand times those watching you see your opponents." This saying expresses *Katachi*.

THE MEANING OF KATA NAMES

Pinan—peace, peaceful, or tranquil mind. The *Pinan* series is comprised of five *Kata* developed by Master Itosu Yatsusune in 1901 to be used as an introductory Karate curriculum for Okinawan middle schools.

Naihanchin (also called *Naihanchi, Naifan, Naifanchin,* and *Dai Po Chin* in Chinese)—horse riding.

Chinto—The Okinawan pronunciation of a Chinese sailor/martial artist's name who, as legend has it, introduced this *Kata* to Okinawa sometime during the 16th century. It should be noted that the characters *(Kanji)* for *Chinto* may be read as "Fighting to the East."

Pasai (also called *Patsai*)—to penetrate a fortress. There are two versions of this *Kata: Dai* (the great) and *Sho* (the small).

Kushanku (also called *Kusanku, Kosokun,* and *Kwanku*)—named for the Chinese attache. There are four versions: *Dai* (the great), *Sho* (the small), *Shiho* (four corner), and *Chibana* named for the first Mayor of Shuri, Okinawa (not to be confused with the famous Karate Master Chibana Choshin [1885–1969]).

Gojushiho (also known as *Gojuy-onbo,* and *Useishi* in the Oki-nawan dialect)—fifty four steps.

Sanchin (also *Saam Chien Quan* in Chinese)—three battles or three conflicts. The name refers to the development of mind, body, spirit, as well as breathing *(Kokyu),* Technique *(Waza)* and stepping *(Hoko).*

Seisan (also called *Seishan)*—thirteen (of Buddhist significance).

Sanseiru (also called *Sanjuroku)*—thirty-six (of Buddhist significance). Calculated by six by six. The first six represent eyes, ears, nose, tongue, body, and spirit. The second six represent color, voice, taste, smell, touch, and justice.

Sepai (also known as *Zattu Pei* in Chinese)—eighteen (of Buddhist significance). Calculated by six by three. The six represent the second six of *Sanseiru.* The three represent good, bad, and peace.

KOEI-KAN KATA

OKINAWAN

SHURI-TE	NAHA-TE
Pinan Shodan	Sanchin
Pinan Nidan	Seisan
Pinan Sandan	Sanseiru
Pinan Yondan	Sepai
Pinan Godan	Suparinpei

Naihanchin Shodan
Naihanchin Nidan
Naihanchin Sandan

Chinto

Passai Sho
Passai Dai

Kushanku Sho
Kushanku Dai
Shiho Kushanku
Chibana Kushanku

Gojushiho

CHINESE

Jaken Ichiro
Renchiken Ichiro

Suparinpei (also called *Peichurin* in the Okinawan dialect)—108 (of Buddhist significance). Calculated by three by thirty-six. The three represent the *Sanchin* and the thirty six the *Sanseiru.* It is based on the Buddhist belief that humankind has 108 evil passions. In Buddhist temples at midnight of the New Year a bell is rung 108 times to drive away these evil passions.

Jaken (Ichiro)—*(She Quan* or *Zheo Chuen* in Mandarin Chinese)—snake fist (No. 1).

Renchiken (Ichiro)—*(Lian Quan* or *Lian Zhi Chuen* in Mandarin Chinese)—Lotus fist (No. 1).

NOTE: It may be that the *Kata* with numerical names (e.g. *Seisan, Sanseiru,* etc.) were thusly named because they were created to practice attacking various groupings of vital anatomical points *(Kyusho)* with a multiplicity of techniques and tactics.

TRAINING HINTS

A. Practice of *Kata* should be done regularly so that its movements can be put to practical use even when out of context. It is useless just to memorize the pattern.

B. Practice *Kata* in slow motion, so that each movement can be fully absorbed.

C. Break the *Kata* down step-by-step, practicing each step individually a number of times.

D. Apply the movements of *Kata* with a partner attacking you. Experiment with variations that could be used in actual combat.

E. Apply the entire *Kata* against multiple attackers.

F. Never rush through *Kata*. Always perform in an exacting fashion.

G. Spend more time on *Kata* that give the greatest difficulty.

H. Give attention to even the most minute details.

I. Each *Kata* should be continually practiced, even after new *Kata* are learned. Never consider yourself done with a particular *Kata*.

NOTES ON THE TRANSMISSION OF KATA

In times past, Masters' selected a particular Kata to be transmitted to general pupils' as a foundational training exercise. After a period of time deemed appropriate by the Master, an individual pupil (one thought to have been proven worthy) was commonly taught a second Kata based on skill, physical stature, and on the techniques contained within said Kata which the Master felt would best suit and enhance the pupil's overall development.

Traditionally, only one pupil was taught the entire syllabus of Kata which made up the Master's system or style. This pupil often became the inheritor of the Master's art. In some cases senior pupils' of a given Master would get together and teach each other the various Kata which they had not been previously taught. In this fashion the entire menu of Kata was learned by senior pupils' who would go on to become Masters' in their own right, and incorporated into their individual teaching curriculums. This situation was, however, not a common one as knowledge was jealousy guarded and vows were often made to Masters' by pupils' in this regard (zealously kept by many). Certain Masters' created new Kata based on their training and research which they felt would open up new avenues and insights to their pupils.' Still others changed the techniques within the original Kata to better fit an individual pupil's needs and to more readily express the practical elements of the Kata or to facilitate transmission to a greater number of pupils.'

NOTES ON THE NUMERIC SYMBOLISM IN KATA NAMES

Within the syllabus of Koei-Kan Kata those with numeric names may be linked to the Buddhist concepts known in Japanese as Hyaku Hachi No Bonno (108 evils/defilements in human nature).

Conceptually (or ideologically) these may be overcome or dispelled through the austere mental and physical training (Shugyo) required in the practice of Karate.

Many Buddhist temples are reached by climbing 108 steps (related to Kata Suparinpei) which are often laid out in two flights of 54 steps each (related to Kata Gojushiho), three flights of 36 steps each (related to Kata Sanseiru), or six flights of 18 steps each (related to Kata Sepai).

The climbing of each step may symbolically represent the elimination of one of the 108 evils which retards the progression of self-improvement or the attainment to ones full potential in the quest to reach enlightenment (Satori in Japanese) at which point one gains a clearer understanding of existence.

10

BOGU

PROTECTIVE ARMOR

The type of *Bogu* (protective armor) used in the *Koei-Kan* system was developed by Onishi Eizo *Kancho Sensei* in 1957 and was tested on March 24th that same year at the Shikoku area Championship of the All-Japan Karate-Do Association, held at the Kenmin-Kan in Matsuyama city. The use of *Bogu* is an integral area of training in *Koei-Kan.* It is not totally unlike the gear worn by European and Japanese fencers. The *Bogu* enables practitioners to apply their techniques with full contact against a moving, thinking opponent. In this fashion a realistic atmosphere exists, which allows practicality and an understanding of effectiveness and efficiency to guide the student in overall development. In all martial entities there is an undeniable need for the reality that actual contact breeds. Without such contact practice often degenerates to a level of swimming on dry land. The necessity of contact has been realized in the martial arts and ways through the ages. Two excellent examples of this can be found in *Kendo* and *Judo.*

Between 1765 A.D. and 1770 A.D. Nakanishi Chuta of Edo (now Tokyo) designed a set of protective armor, which was the forerunner of today's *Kendo* gear. It was used in conjunction with a type of dummy sword known as Shinai¦ made of bamboo strips, which allowed for a certain "give" when contact was made. This greatly enhanced the practitioner's training and ability because positive conclusions could be drawn as to the significance of techniques. Around 1882 Kano Jigoro (1860–1938) began to make popular his new martial system, which he named *Judo.* In this system Kano made use of a special type of *Tatami* (straw mat) to enable students to throw each other with full force repeatedly during practice. This differed greatly from many of the earlier schools of Jujutsu, which trained on hardwood floors. From these examples we can clearly see the beneficial possibilities that can be derived from the use of *Bogu.*

1972 All Japan Koei-Kan Karate-Do Championship, Kamata Sports Stadium, Tokyo (author on left).

PARTS OF THE BOGU

1. *Men*—helmet
2. *Do*—chest protector
3. *Te*—gloves
4. Others— A) *Kintekiate*—groin cup
   B) *Suneate*—shin protector

---

1. The use of a wooden sword (termed *Bokken)* during training allowed practitioners to engage in contests with a lesser mortality rate than did the use of a live blade (Shinken). However, the hard wooden *Bokken* often caused serious injury and sometimes death.

   For this reason Nakanishi Chuta, a follower of Ono Jirouemon (founder of the Nakanishi Itto-Ryu School of Swordsmanship) developed a type of hand and forearm protector *(Kote),* and redesigned the *Shinai.*
2. *Jujutsu* (or *Jujitsu)* sometimes called *Yawara* in ancient times, was the forerunner of *Judo.*

11

EXAMINATION OF RANK AND GRADE

A n examination *(Shinsa)* or test *(Shiken)* in the *Koei-Kan* system is meant to teach the trainee what is not known, as opposed to that which is known. In this way the student can strive to reach higher goals.

Karate-Do is a search for self improvement *(Kaizen)* through the constant forging of one's mind, body, and spirit. *Karate-Do* as with the human soul, is like a bottomless well. We can never plumb its depth.

The importance lies in the journey, not in the destination. The heart of the examination is in the examination of oneself, not in the judgment of others. The person makes the worth of the grade, not the grade the worth of the person. The attaining of the grade is but a higher step upon the ladder of life. It is important to climb to that rung that fulfills one's self.

Karate-Do will allow each individual to go to that level that he or she wishes to attain.

It is hoped that the practitioner will continue to seek improvement throughout life in order to achieve a happier, healthier, and more peaceful and prosperous existence.

An examination consists of written, oral, and physical parts based on the general curriculum *(Kyoka)* of the system. After the examination, a formal announcement *(Happyo)* and explanation *(Kaisetsu)* of the test results are given.

A BRIEF BACKGROUND OF RANK AND GRADE

The *Kyu* (ranks below black belt) and *Dan* (black belt grades) system was initiated by Master Kano Jigoro (1860–1938) the founder of *Judo.* One version states that Master Kano, seeing the need to differentiate between teachers and students, began using a black sash (the type used with a Japanese kimono) to be worn by his advanced pupils. It is believed that around 1907 the sash was replaced by the *Kuro Obi* (black belt). As time went on a brown belt was instituted to designate that further classified pupils into *Shoshinsha* (beginner), *Chukyusha* (mid-level/intermediate), *Jokyusha* (upper-level/advanced) and *Yudansha* (black belt/advanced, with ascending grades). Eventually various belt colors were used to distinguish the different levels of achievement. The *Kyu/Dan* system was carried over to *Karate-Do* after its introduction into mainland Japan from Okinawa, most notably by Master Funakoshi (Tominakoshi) Gichin (1868–1957).

The original belt color system used in *Koei-Kan* was white belt (*Shiro Obi)*, brown belt *(Cha Obi),* and black belt *(Kuro Obi).* The brown belt was and is divided into three levels: *San-Kyu, Ni-Kyu,* and *I-Kyu* (or *Ichi-Kyu). San-Kyu* is the lowest and *I-Kyu* is the highest. The black belt is divided into eight levels, *Shodan* (first grade or step) being the lowest and *Hachidan* (eighth grade) being the highest. In 1972 Onishi *Kancho Sensei* granted permission for the use of the green belt *(Midori Obi)* outside of Japan.

All black belt grades above *Godan* (fifth grade) are honorary and are based on time, contribution to the furtherance of the art, and past performance.

NOTE: All ranks under black belt are termed *Mudansha.* Black belt ranks are termed *Yudansha.*

A BRIEF BACKGROUND OF TITLES

The use of certain titles to designate rank, station, or status has been used in the classical martial arts *(Bugei* or *Bujutsu)* of Japan since ancient times. The use of titles in the more modern *Budo* (martial ways) was given official recognition with the establishment of the Dai Nippon Butokukai (Japan Great Martial Virtue Association) in Kyoto in April 1895. The Butokukai was sanctioned by the government to regulate and standardize the various *Budo* and *Bugei Ryu* (schools/systems) and to issue *Menjo* (certificates) and *Menkyo* (licenses). The three original titles of *Hanshi, Kyoshi,* and *Renshi* were introduced in this fashion, and other titles were subsequently introduced.

TITLES

There are many titles and terms that are used to designate rank, grade, or position in the Japanese martial arts and ways (Bugei/Bujutsu and Budo, respectively). Some are frequently used, while others are archaic and rarely implemented at the present time.

It should be noted that titles are generally used in the written rather than the spoken language as a means of listing one's credentials.

A good analogy would be the title M.D. (medical doctor) for a physician, or the academic titles Ph.D., M.A., B.S., M.S., etc.

In the Japanese martial arts and ways it is traditionally considered pretentious to refer to these titles when making a spoken reference to a high-ranking practitioner.

Furthermore, there are certain titles used strictly for technical classification purposes and not used to address another.

TITLES AND TERMS OF RANK AND GRADE

Chukyusha—One of middle level. An intermediate. In the *Kyu* ranks.

Dai Hyosha—A headmaster, a critic, or reviewer.

Dai Sensei or *O sensei*—Great teacher.

Dan—A step (as on a ladder). A level. A grade. Used to describe a grade or grades of black belt.

Dohai—One of equal training rank and/or time.

Dojo Cho—Head of a *Dojo.*

Hanshi—Model person. Highest level. Master teacher or teacher of teachers. Title given at *Hachidan* (eighth Dan) and above.

Ho—This is a contraction of the word *Hobo* (nearly). Sometimes used to denote a probationary grade (e.g., *Shodan-Ho).*

Jokyusha—One of upper level in the *Kyu* ranks.

Kaicho—Chairman.

Kancho—Hall president or chief. Headmaster of a system or style.

Kensei—First saint. A title sometimes used to describe a practitioner of legendary stature.

Kohai—Behind companion. A junior in training rank and/or time.
   Note: Although *Senpai* is a proper form of address for one's senior, *Kohai* should not be used as a spoken title.

Kyosei—Student teacher. *Shodan* level.

Kyoshi—A title or level generally equated with *Rokudan/Shichidan* (sixth or seventh *Dan*).

Kyu—Rank under black belt.

Meijin—A wise person, a great Master. A wizard. This is a title that denotes the ultimate in the Japanese martial arts and ways. One that is the pinnacle of a field.

Mudansha—One who holds a rank under black belt.

Renshi—Forging person. A title or level generally equated with *Yondan/Godan* (fourth or fifth *Dan*).

Saiko Shihan—Absolute Master. Supreme Advisor.

Senpai—Previous companion. One's senior in training rank and/or time.
Note: Seniors should be addressed by this title.

Sensei—Previously born. One who has gone before. A title of respect for one's wisdom. Generally used to describe a teacher.

Shi—Master

Shidoin or *Fukushidoin*—A lower-lever instructor. A title generally equated with *Nidan/Sandan* (second or third *Dan*).

Shihan—A Master. A senior or upper-level instructor. A model for others. A title or level generally equated with *Godan/Rokudan* (fifth or sixth *Dan*) and sometimes *Shichidan* (seventh *Dan*).

Shihan Dai—Top assistant. Second in the teaching line of command.

Shinan—Guide/teacher. A term derived from a type of Chinese compass that always pointed south; the significance being that the teacher always lead the pupil in the correct direction.

Shoshinsha—A beginner.

Soke—The hereditary headmaster of a system or style *(Ryu)*. Usually passed on within a family from generation to generation.

Soke Dai—Heir apparent to a system or style.

Sosai—President or Governor.

Soshi, Shiso, Kaiso, or *Shuso*—Founder (of a system or style).

Yudansha—One who holds a grade of black belt.

NOTE: A certificate of rank or grade is termed Menjo. A license is termed Menkyo. A teaching license is termed Kyoju Dairi. A license of full proficiency (or final teachings) is termed Menkyo Kaiden. An international instructor's certificate is termed Kokusai Shihan Menkyo.

TERMS USED TO DESCRIBE STUDENTS/DISCIPLES

Ani Deshi—A senior disciple.

Kaikin Deshi—A disciple who never misses class.

Kenshusei—Trainee Instructor.

Mago Deshi—A disciple of one's disciple.

Mana Deshi—A favorite pupil.

Montei/Monjin—Disciple.

Seito—Pupil/Student.

Shosei—Student dependent. Similar to *Uchi Deshi.* Sometimes used to describe the
most senior or top student.

Uchi Deshi—A live-in disciple.

> NOTE: There are many more terms used to describe rank and grade, but these will give a good
> general base.

12

Heigo

Military Terminology

Japanese terminology is used in the *Koei-Kan* system because it is the native language of the country where the system was founded and developed. This procedure is commonly followed in the oriental martial arts and ways because the technical terminology used serves as a universal method of communication between the practitioners of a given system, so that they may train together, even though they may speak different languages. This is similar to the use of Latin among physicians. Furthermore, a cursory understanding of the mother tongue of the country of origin of an art gives one a more cogent feel for the culture that spawned said art, thus allowing a greater insight into its deeper meanings. It is also true that many terms and phrases "lose something in translation" from one language to another.

The mastery of a different language will certainly not increase one's skill in combat, but it can serve as a mental exercise in becoming more aware of deeper meanings of an art.

It is important to keep in mind that much of the terminology used is peculiar to the martial arts and ways of Japan and may have little meaning to native Japanese speakers outside of this context. The best example of this is the word *Osu*, which is pronounced with the "U" being silent. The word *Osu* originated during the later part of the Tokugawa (or Edo) era as a greeting among Samurai, and acquired wide usage in later years throughout Karate Dojo where it was thought of as a contraction of *Osu Shinobu*. (*Osu*—to push, *Shinobu*—to endure, to be patient). In this context *Osu* may be taken to mean "Push harder and endure" or "Be patient and try harder."

Osu continues to be used as a military greeting among many Karate practitioners and in some cases is even used as an affirmation, meaning "I understand" or "yes."

While some *Heigo* expressions have no meaning to those outside the martial arts and ways, others are merely modified or contracted versions of common Japanese. Examples of this would be *Ha* used in place of *Hai* (yes) and *Yosh* used in place of *Yoroshiie* (good, fine, right, okay). Also the word *Kiotsuke* (line up), which is a contraction of the word *Kiotsukete* (be careful, beware, be alert). Another such word (or interjection) is *Sa,* meaning "well" or "let's go." It is said to an opponent prior to combat to demonstrate a strong spirit or willingness to "mix it up."

Everyday Japanese words and phrases are also used in the practice of the martial arts and ways, as well as a purely *Heigo* vocabulary. In either case, during training, terminology is pronounced in a forceful fashion. This is to express strength and sincerity.

It should be further noted that there may be more than one term (e.g. *Juji Uke*— cross block or *Kosa Uke*—intersecting block) that describes the same technique, principle, thought, etc. This is often simply a matter of preference on the part of a particular school.

As a basic rule of thumb when speaking Japanese, the vowels are pronounced as in Spanish and the consonants almost always as in English. Double consonants like the "pp" in Nippon are pronounced like the p sounds that connect two words in English, like "flip past."

The vowels "I" and "U" are sometimes short; that is, they are not voiced or pronounced at all.

Most Japanese nouns do not make a distinction between the singular and the plural. For example, "Sensei" may mean both "teacher" and "teachers."

VOWELS

A—Sounds like "AH" as the "A" in Father
I—Sounds like "EE" as the "I" in Machine
U—Sounds like "OO" as the "U" in Flu
E—Sounds like "EH" as the "A" in Ate
O—Sounds like "OH" as the "O" in Open

I have added some useful daily expressions in Japanese for those who may wish to further their knowledge of the language.

GENERAL TERMS

Aite—An opponent.

Atama/Karada Fure—Head/body touch. An exercise to develop skill in dodging.

Atemi/Atemi Waza—The art of striking vital points. Techniques for striking vital points.

Deshi/Seito—Disciple/student or pupil.

Dogu—Training equipment for *Budo.*

Doshi—One's Dojo mates.

Honbun—One's duty (or duties) as a pupil.

Hongi—True meaning. The most important principle of a technique.

Ifu (or *Kofu)*—A *Dojo* tradition.

Karate (Ka)—A Karate practitioner.

Katate—One hand.

Kawashi (Waza)—Dodging (techniques).

Kerihanashi (Kehanashi or *Kebanashi)*—A returning kick. A snap kick.

Kerikomi (or *Kekomi)*—A thrust kick.

Kobudo/Kobujutsu—Ancient Okinawan weapons arts. Also called *Bukiho* (or *Tegua*—small hands) in the Okinawan dialect of *Hogen* A.K.A. *Hogan.* The five most common weapons are:

>*Bo (Rokushakubo)*—six foot staff.
>
>*Sai*—Short trident (used in pairs).
>
>*Tonfa*—Mill wheel handle (used in pairs).
>
>*Kama*—Sickle. Known as Nichogama when used in pairs (as is the common practice).
>
>*Nunchaku*—Flail.

Mae Ashi—Front leg/foot (when standing in a fighting stance).

Maete—Front hand (when standing in a fighting stance).

Maita—Submission (I submit).

Mitorigeiko—The practice of observation. The ability to observe and then apply a technique.

Obi Musubi—The knot on a belt.

Obi Tori—Techniques using the belt. (also an exercise used to develop skill in dodging).

Ritsudo—The rhythm of *Kata.*

Ryote—Both hands (2 hands)

Seme—Attack, attacker, initiator of an attack.

Suki—An opening in an opponents defense (also *Kaimon*—open gate).

Shitei Kata or *Shinko Kata*—Designated *Kata* (*Kata* required for grading).

Tokui (Waza/Kata)—Favorite (technique/form).

Uke—Block, defend. The receiver of an attack.

Ushiro Ashi—Rear leg/foot (when in a fighting stance).

Ushirote—Rear hand (when in a fighting stance).

Yudanshakai—An organization of black belts.

USEFUL DAILY EXPRESSIONS

Ohayo Gozaimasu—Good morning.

Konichi Wa—Good afternoon.

Konban Wa—Good evening.

Oyasumi Nasai—Good night.

Matta or *Matta Aimasho*—See you or see you again.

O Daijini—Take care of yourself.

Kiotsukete—Take care or be careful.

Sayonara—Goodbye

Domo Arigato Gozaimasu (or *Gozaimashita*)—Thank you very much.

Do Itashimashite—You're welcome.

Gomen Nasai—Excuse me.

Sumimasen—Pardon me/excuse me.

Wakarimasu Ka?—Do you understand?

Wakarimasu or *Wakaru*—I understand.

Wakarimasen or *Wakarunai*—I don't understand.

Hai—Yes.

Iie—No.

Onamae Wa?—What's your name?

Hajimemashite—How do you do?

Dozo Yoroshiku—Please to meet you.

Ogenki Desu Ka?—How are you? (literally: Are you healthy?)

Genki Desu—I'm fine.

Chotto Matte Kudasai—Just a moment please.

Shitsurei Shimasu—I'm sorry.

Daijobu—Okay

Ii Desu—Good

Dame Desu—Bad

Dozo—Please

COUNTING IN JAPANESE

In the Dojo counting is almost always done on a one-to-ten basis; however, as a point of reference and for those who wish to go beyond the basic framework of counting, I have extended the procedure. It should be noted that counting cadence is somewhat of a skill, in that it dictates the pace and intensity of training.

Ichi	1	*Ju Ichi*	11
Ni	2	*Ju Ni*	12
San	3	*Ju San*	13
Shi	4	*Ju Shi*	14
Go	5	*Ju Go*	15
Roku	6	*Ju Roku*	16
Shichi	7	*Ju Shichi*	17
Hachi	8	*Ju Hachi*	18
Ku	9	*Ju Ku*	19
Ju	10	*Ni Ju*	20

To continue counting beyond twenty add *Ichi, Ni,* etc., to *Ni Ju.* The same process is followed as the count ascends.

San Ju	30	*Ku Ju* (or *Kyu Ju*)	90
Yon Ju	40	*Hyaku*	100
Go Ju	50	*Sen*	1,000
Roku Ju	60	*Man*	10,000
Shichi Ju	70	*Ju Man*	100,000
Hachi Ju	80	*Hyaku Ju Man*	1,000,000

FUNDAMENTAL TRAINING COMMANDS AND TERMS

Gambatte—Try harder (do your best).

Gorei—To act on command.

Gorei Nashi—Command to do *Kata* without counts (on the call of *Hajime).*

Hai—Yes (an affirmation).

Hajime—Begin or start.

Hantai—Change sides (from left to right).

Hayaku—A command to move rapidly.

Iie—No.

Kamae—To fix into guard position.

Karuku—A command to move lightly with correct motion.

Kawaru (or *Kaette)*—To change (to change partners or attack and defense positions).

Kiritsu (or *Tatsu)*—Stand.

Matte—Pause (from an action).

Mawaru (or *Mawatte)*—Pivot, turn, or rotate.

Mo Ichido—Repeat

Mo Ikkae—Once again.

Modotte—Return to original position.

Mukai Atte—A command to pair off.

Naotte—To relax and catch ones breath.

Onaji—Same (Do the same technique).

Rei—Bow

Suwarinasai*—Sit *(Agura* or *Seiza).*

Tsuyoku—A command to move with strength.

Wakare—To break (formation, a clinch, etc.).

Yame—Stop or end.

Yasume—Rest

Yoi—A command to make ready.

Yowaku—A command to move lightly.

Yukuri—A command to move slowly.

---

*Agura—Informal seated posture (legs crossed). *Seiza*—Formal seated posture (legs tucked under).

DIRECTIONAL AND AREA TERMS

Mae (Ni)—Forward or front. A command to move forward.

Yoko (Ni)—Side. A command to move sideways.

Ushiro (Ni)—Rear or back. A command to move backwards.

Naname or *Hasu (Ni)*—Diagonal. A command to move on a diagonal.

Mawaru or *Mawatte (Ni)*—Turn or pivot (a command to turn or pivot).

Ue—Up

Shita—Down

Migi—Right

Hidari—Left

Uchi—Inside

Soto—Outside

Omote—Outer (the surface, the obverse)

Ura—Reverse (the other side)

Jodan—Upper level

Chudan—Middle level

Gedan—Lower level

Tate—Vertical

Suihei—Horizontal

Chokusen (Ni)—Straight line (a command to move in a straight line)

Nidan—Bi-level

Otoshi—Dropping (downward)

CHART OF DIRECTION

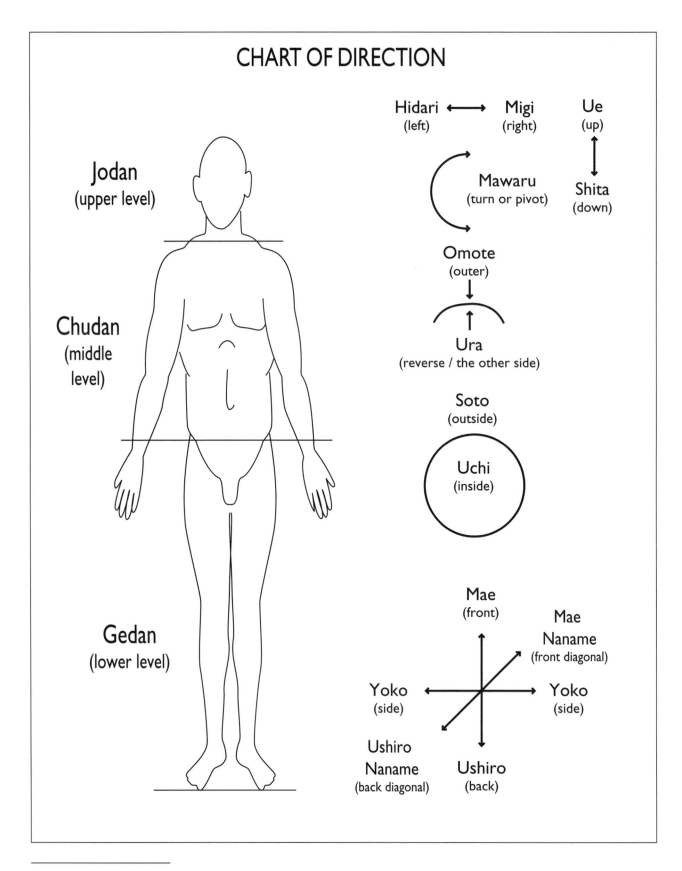

Jodan
(upper level)

Chudan
(middle level)

Gedan
(lower level)

Hidari ←→ Migi
(left)   (right)

Ue
(up)

Mawaru
(turn or pivot)

Shita
(down)

Omote
(outer)

Ura
(reverse / the other side)

Soto
(outside)

Uchi
(inside)

Mae
(front)

Mae
Naname
(front diagonal)

Yoko
(side)

Yoko
(side)

Ushiro
Naname
(back diagonal)

Ushiro
(back)

CONTEST (SHIAI) TERMS

Aiuchi—Simultaneous attack: no point.

Aka—Red

Aka No Kachi—Victory red.

Atoshibaraku—Thirty second warning until end of match.

Awasete Ippon—Two half points equaling one full point.

Chui (Hansoku Chui)—Warning (warning of a foul).

Chuoi Modoru—Return to center of contest area.

Encho—Prolonging time of match (overtime).

Fukushin Shugo—Calling together of judges for consultation.

Fusen—Default

Hajime—Begin

Hansoku—Foul

Hansokumake—Loss by foul.

Hantei—Decision

Hatta—Flag

Hikiwake—A draw.

Ippon—Full point.

Ippon Shobu—One point contest.

Ippongachi—One point win.

Jikan—Time

Jogai—Out of bounds.

Jogai Nakae—Call to contestants to return to the contest area.

Matte—Pause

Nihon Shobu—Two point contest

Saiten—Point scoring system.

Sanbon Shobu—Three point contest

Shiaijo—Contest area.

Shikakumake—Loss by disqualification.

Shimpan—Referee

Shiro—White

Shiro No Kachi—Victory white.

Shobu—Contest (match).

Shushin—Judge

Taikai—A championship, a tournament, a demonstration.

Taryu Shiai (or *Taryu Taikai*)—A contest between different styles/systems (or championship/tournament between different styles/systems).

Waza Ari—One-half a point.

Yame—Stop

TARGET AREAS

Tobu—Head area.
Ganmen—Facial area.
Keibu—Neck area
Kyobu—Chest area.
Fukubu—Diaphragm, abdomen and side of the chest area.
Haibu—Back area.

There are many more terms that may be applied to Karate contests depending upon the rules which are implemented. However, the aforementioned terms are commonly used and will give a cursory idea of contest terminology.

13

MON AND MONSHO

CRESTS AND PATCHES

Crests, patches, emblems, and insignias have traditionally and historically been used in the martial arts and ways to represent various groups, arts, divisions, ranks, grades, etc.

In *Koei-Kan Karate-Do* two crests are predominantly utilized. The first is the cherry blossom *(Sakura)*. This crest was adopted as the symbol of the All-Japan Karatedo Association (Zen Nihon Karatedo Renmei) founded by Master Toyama Kanken in 1946. Official permission was given by Onishi Eizo Kancho Sensei in 1971 to use the cherry blossom as the representative emblem of *Koei-Kan* outside of Japan.

The symbolic use of the cherry blossom can be traced back in Japanese history to the early written classics *Kojiki* and *Nihon Shoki*. Around the tenth century the cherry blossom came to be thought of as a sort of the "national flower." The statement "In flowers the cherry blossom. In men the samurai" may give some indication as to the status of the cherry blossom crest.

The second emblem/crest utilized in *Koei-Kan* is the paulownia *(Kiri)*. This is the leaf of the paulownia tree *(Shinobibai)*.

The paulownia crest and the chrysanthemum *(Kiku)* are considered dual symbols of the Japanese imperial throne. This association was crystallized during the early thirteenth century. At that time Emperor Godaigo conferred both of these crests upon the founder of the Ashikaga line of Shogun (Ashikaga Takauji), who in turn conferred the right to bear the paulownia crest upon certain *Daimyo** who were loyal to the Shogun and the Emperor. This custom was carried on by Toyotomi Hideyoshi in the late sixteenth century.

It was by this process that the Onishi family (through their ancestral Samurai clan, the Oshimiki) obtained the use of the paulownia crest.

Koei-Kan Patch (Monsho)

*Daimyo—First name. A title given to a class of feudal land barons.

Go Hichi (shichi) Kiri Crest (Mon)

There are many forms of the paulownia crest. The most common is termed *Kiri Go San.* This form is symbolized by the configuration of three blooms on either side of five blooms that top the major portion of the leaf.

The type that is used as the Onishi family crest is termed *Go Hichi* (or *Shichi) Kiri,* which consists of five blooms on either side of seven blooms that top the major portion of the leaf.

CRESTS AND PATCHES USED TO DESIGNATE RANK AND GRADE

Cherry blossom *(Sakura)*—used for general members.

Koei-Kan **in the form of black** *Kanji* **(Japanese characters)**—used to designate the grades of first- and second-degree black belt.

Koei-Kan **in the form of red** *Kanji* **(Japanese characters)**—used to designate the grade of third- and fourth-degree black belt.

Kendo Gaku **in the form of black** *Kanji* **(Japanese characters)**—used to designate fifth- and sixth-degree black belt.

Kendo Gaku **in the form of red** *Kanji* **(Japanese characters)**—used to designate seventh- and eighth-degree black belt.

14

Heiho

Strategy

In all martial entities strategy is imperative. When, how, where, and why are, and have been, crucial elements both mentally and physically in the success of offense and defense during battle. A good *Heihojin* (strategist) makes a good warrior. Martial arts and ways are a microcosm of life, and as such the elements described here may be applied to life in general. The following information is but a brief examination and definition of certain basic principles that are relative to the practice and precepts of *Koei-Kan Karate-Do* and the *Budo* in general.

Fudoshin—Immovable mind/spirit. An attitude or state of mind that is imperturbable, focused, and undistracted from achieving one's goal. Also see the sections on *Kata* and *Budo.*

Go No Sen—To counterattack with correct timing and technique.

Hakari—Balance. This may relate not only to being physically balanced, but also to being balanced in all areas of life.

Haragei (**also** *Genshin*)—Intuition. *Hara* may be defined as "stomach" or "abdomen." *Gei* may be defined as an "art or craft." Haragei may therefore be termed the "Art of the stomach or abdomen." In Japanese thought the idea has been traditionally promulgated that the mind, heart, and soul of a human being lies in an area known as *Saika Tanden* (an area between the navel and the groin), sometimes more specifically called *Itten* (the one point). It is commonly believed that the *Ki* (intrinsic energy) emanates from this spot. Through proper training a practitioner may develop a keen intuitive or sixth sense that allows one to perceive an attack before it is launched and act accordingly. Furthermore, at a higher level, ability in *Haragei* may even enable the practitioner to avoid confrontation before the situation exists. This type of intuition is often called in Western terms "a gut feeling."

Hen-O—The correct response to a given attack.

Ikken Hisatsu—One blow or a one-point kill. This is the principle of launching each attack with such precision and focus that it is potentially the coup de grace. The decisive, finishing blow. *Ikken Hisatsu* is both a strategy and an attitude. It applies to both combat and day-to-day training. It is especially important to train with the goal of developing the ability to end a battle with one technique.

In/Yo (Known in Chinese as Yin/Yang)—The positive and negative principles of nature. This may represent hard/soft, male/female, good/evil, plus/minus, etc. The basic idea behind the *In/Yo* principle is a universal balance of opposites. To be able to blend, meld, and flow with the ups and downs of life lies at the heart of In and Yo. This relates to *Rinkiohen* (adaptability to all circumstances) and to the idea of harmony, peace, and enlightenment through flowing with things.

➤ See also the section on Budo (Wa/Peace).

Karate Ni Sente Nashii—"There is no first attack in Karate." This phrase, popularized by the Karate Master Funakoshi Gichin (Tominakoshi Gichin in the Okinawan dialect) is often mistaken to mean that one should only react physically when physically attacked. This is somewhat erroneous. The spirit expressed in this saying is that one should not act in an aggressive fashion but should be prepared to take action when acted against aggressively. An example of this would be if one were confronted with an assailant wielding a weapon; even if the assailant has not actually attacked, the attitude of aggression has already taken place, thus requiring appropriate response. This strategy is imperative to survival. By waiting for an actual attack to be launched, one is in jeopardy of defeat. A person should always avoid confrontation but never fear a righteous response to such an unavoidable confrontation. In the Japanese martial arts and ways the word _Ma_ is usually thought of as one's personal "space" an area which others do not invade without invitation. The Samurai had a code that included *Saya Ate* (scabbard attack). If the scabbard of one Samurai touched another's in passing, a duel of honor had to take place. This relates to _Ma_. Each of us has a certain space in life that must be respected. In summary: A practitioner of martial arts should never hide behind the principle of non-aggression when positive action must be taken to stand up for what is correct.

➤ See also the section on Kata.

Kawashi—To integrate with the opponent's attack in order to affect a counter attack.

Keikaku—Planning. This form of strategy implies the idea of visualization or imaging. Picturing in one's mind a combative situation prior to occurrence can be a useful tool. Playing out one's response and actions in a situation in one's mind before the actual (to use a colloquialism) "show-down" is often helpful in survival. Examples of this type of strategy may be found in games of Western origin, such as billiards and chess and in Japanese games such as *Go* and *Shogi*. "Playing position" is often the key to success, especially when dealing with more than one opponent. It should, however, be kept in mind that this principle is only a viable strategy when one is placed in a position whereby you are taken by surprise and don't have the opportunity to avoid the situation but have the time to plan. A prime example of this is when one is placed in a corner, unable to exit, and verbal exchange occurs, as opposed to the proverbial "sucker-punch," which is immediate.

Kuzushi—To unbalance. This may be construed as a form of the Japanese word *Kuzusu* (to pull down or to crumble). This principle relates to both the physical and psychological attitude of unbalancing the opponent. This may be accomplished on a physical level by grabbing, pulling, pushing, faking, etc., thus making the opponent move in such a fashion as to put him/her in a position of unbalance (e.g., one hip/shoulder higher than the other, making the opponent shift body weight in a desired direction, etc.). On a psychological level *Kuzushi* may be achieved through the employment of what may be termed "psyching-out" the opponent by way of a stare, the display of a strong, calm attitude, etc.

Maai—Combative engagement distance. This refers to the distance between you and your opponent. There are three fundamental ranges: *Toma* (long range), and *Uchima* (striking range/sometimes called *Chuma* [mid-range]), and *Chikama* (close range). The strategy for each depends on a variety of variables, such as one's physical stature, the stature of one's opponent, the number of opponents, the strength, weakness and level of skill of the opposition, etc.

Metsuke—Point of observation. This refers to the area upon which one's gaze is fixed. There are many theories and strategies concerning this principle.

Mizu No Kokoro—Mind like water. This principle refers to being calm *(Shizuka Na)* at all times. This is particularly important during combat. An undisturbed pool of water will reflect a clear and true image. If the pool is disturbed, the image will be distorted. This principle is of the utmost importance. If the mind and spirit are not calm, correct responses will not be enacted. One must overcome fears and trepidations in order to be able to perform at an optimal combative level. The principle of *Mizu No Kokoro* also relates to the state of *Mushin* (the nothing mind).

➤ See also the section on *Budo.*

Mushin—The nothing mind. This principle relates to a state of mind where one is without preconception, which is conducive to reflex action. To act and react calmly is a great attribute in the *Budo* (and in life in general). In combat a state of calmness is of the utmost importance. It is not the swiftest but the most deliberate and focused sword that cuts the deepest. "Act in haste, repent in leisure." By developing *Mushin* one is able to attain a clear and quick assessment of any given situation (perspicacity) and respond accordingly. Outside of its obvious combative value, a more mundane benefit lies in the alleviation of day-to-day stress. On the subject of *Mushin,* the legendary Japanese swordsman Miyamoto Musashi (1582–1645) wrote, "Under the sword lifted high there is hell making you tremble; but go ahead and you have the land of bliss," thus illustrating the role of *Mushin* in overcoming fear.

➤ See also *Mizu No Kokoro* and the sections on *Budo, Kata* and the meaning of Karate.

Riai—Timing. I believe The phrase "Timing is everything" aptly expresses a key not only to combat but to life itself.

Ri/Ji—The universal laws of nature and their applications. This is a principle found in Japanese arts, religions, etc. Fundamentally, *Ji* is the expression or application of *Ri* (the laws of nature) through action. In the *Budo* a practitioner strives to master himself/herself through the mastery of technique following the laws of nature. It is through this mastery that one attains individual and spontaneous application of one's art in all situations. To control without (consciously) controlling is at the core of this principle. In a deeper sense, this principle also implies an acceptance of nature's laws (i.e., better life and death) thus preparing us to face the inevitable. As practitioners of the martial ways we attempt to overcome our fears through training. In times past the Samurai utilized this principle (through necessity) to help overcome their natural fear of death in combat which confronted them daily. Many sought comfort not only in their military training, but in religious faith in Buddhism and/or Shintoism. Regardless of religious or philosophical belief, the *Ri/Ji* principle may be constructively applied to enhance one's existence.

➤ See also *Daiojo* and *Shu Ha Ri.*

Sasoi Waza—Allurement techniques. To purposely leave openings in one's defense to draw the opponent in.

Sen—To take the initiative. To attack. To be the aggressor.

Sen No Sen—To take the initiative from the initiator. To attack the attack. This refers to the idea that when an attack is launched an opening of some sort is created for an instant. At that instant one launches one's own attack to that opening before the completion of the original technique. This is considered a high-level strategy.

Sutemi Waza—Sacrifice techniques. This strategy relates to putting oneself in a vulnerable position in order to gain an advantage through the element of surprise.

Tokon—Fighting spirit (sometimes called *Konjo*/mercenary spirit). A tenacious attitude. An intestinal fortitude. To go forward regardless of circumstance and endure, regardless of pain and injury. "Respect all. Fear none."

➤ Also see section on *Kata.*

Tokoshi—Methods and strategies for closing the gap between you and your opponent.

Tsuki No Kokoro—Mind like the moon. This principle stresses the necessity of being aware of the totality of all things. More specifically, the intentions and actions of the opponent. Just as a full, unclouded moon shines on the totality of an object, one should always be alert to the entire situation

Tsumeru—To completely stop and/or control an oncoming attack.

Zanshin (remaining spirit)—This principle alludes to a state of alertness after the execution and completion of a technique. There is a saying that exemplifies this concept. "The dead tiger kills the most hunters." This fundamentally implies that one should never let one's guard down, even after it seems that the opponent has been vanquished. A good example of this principle may be found in the execution of traditional *Kata.* After the completion of a technique or combination of techniques, there is often a pause. At this point a heightened sense of awareness takes place, and a correct assessment of the situation occurs, allowing for proper action to be implemented.

15

KI, KIAI, KIME

KI ➤ Intrinsic Energy / Life-Force

Ki may be basically thought of as the intrinsic energy found in all living things. The healthier and stronger the being, the greater the level of *Ki*. The level of *Ki* is further increased in proportion to one's ability to unify the mind, body and spirit, thus achieving a "oneness." A balanced life force, functioning at optimal efficiency.

Through training *Ki* may be channeled in such a way as to achieve feats beyond the norm; however, it should never be over-encumbered in mysticism. It is interesting to note that *Ki* is a suffix in Japanese words such as *Denki* (electricity) and *Byoki* (sick or ill, i.e., weak *Ki)* and a prefix in words such as *Kimochi* (feeling or sensation).

KIAI ➤ Spirit Letting or Super Power

Kiai is often defined as spirit letting or superpower. This is, however, a somewhat erroneous definition. The Japanese word *Kiai* is composed of two Japanese characters *(Kanji)*. Ki is defined as "intrinsic energy" and Ai is a contraction of the word *awaseru*, which means "to unite." *Kiai* is an intensification of *Ki* at a given instant. It may at times take the form of a scream or yell. This aids in muscle contraction (through breath exhalation) and the release of adrenaline into the bloodstream. On a psychological level *Kiai* may bolster the spirit of the user and demoralize the spirit of the one it is used against.

There is also a silent *Kiai,* which may take the form of a soundless exhalation of breath or just a manual tensing of muscles. *Kiai* may be a state of mind. It may be said that a person has *Kiai* when said person exudes a strong, imperturbable presence.

Kiai occurs naturally. The sympathetic nervous system is brought into play automatically during periods of fear, anger, flight, fright, and sexual activity, thus releasing adrenaline.

A classic example of natural *Kiai* is when an average human being performs an above-average or seemingly impossible task during times of crisis e.g., a mother lifting an automobile off her child after an accident. This is an extension of subconscious *Kiai*. The practitioner of the martial arts and ways attempts, through training, to achieve various levels of *Ki* on a conscious level at appropriate times, e.g., during combat.

KIME ◆ Focus

Kime is a contraction of the Japanese word *Kimeru,* which means to "fix decisively." This principle refers to instantaneously concentrating all one's energy on a given point at a given moment, both physically and psychologically. The ultimate goal is to achieve maximum power. Ones entire being must work in harmony at the exact instant of impact. Physical aspects such as velocity, torque, muscle contraction, exhalation, correct motion of technique, etc., play a key role in focus.

Psychologically, a mind set of follow-through to completion must be conjunctively applied. Upon said completion an immediate return to a state of relaxation occurs, allowing preparation for subsequent action to take place.

➤ See also section on *Kata.*

ANATOMY

KAIBO GAKU

GENERAL PARTS OF THE BODY

1. Head—*Atama*
2. Face—*Kao*
3. Eyes—*Me*
4. Ears—*Mimi*
5. Nose—*Hana*
6. Mouth / Lips—*Kuchi / Kuchibiru*
7. Chin—*Ago* (or *Shita Ago)*
8. Throat—*Nodo*
9. Neck—*Kubi*
10. Shoulders—*Kata*
11. Arm—*Ude*
12. Elbow—*Hiji*
13. Forearm—*Kote* (or *Zenwan*)
14. Wrist—*Tekubi*
15. Hand—*Te*
16. Palm—*Shotei*
17. Thumb—*Oya Yubi*
18. Finger(s)—*Te No Yubi*
19. Chest—*Mune* or *Kyobu*
20. Stomach / Abdominal Region—*Hara / Fukubu*
21. Hips—*Koshi*
22. Back—*Senaka*
23. Leg(s) / Foot (Feet)—*Ashi*
24. Thigh—*Momo*
25. Knee / Kneecap—*Hiza / Hizagashira*
26. Shin—*Mukozune* or *Sune*
27. Calf—*Fukura Hagi*

28. Ankle—*Ashi Kubi*
29. Toe(s)—*Ashi Yubi*

LIST OF KIHON KYUSHO

1. *Tento*—crown of head
2. *Komekami*—the temple
3. *Miken*—the summit of the nose in center of forehead
4. *Gansei*—the eyeball
5. *Mimi*—the ear
6. *Seidon*—area above and below the eyes
7. *Bito*—bridge of the nose
8. *Hanagashira*—base or tip of nose
9. *Jinchu*—spot below base of nose (the philtrum)
10. *Gekon*—spot beneath the lower lip
11. *Mikazuki*—the jaw
12. *Ago*—the chin
13. *Shofu*—side of the neck
14. *Sonu*—the Adams apple
15. *Hichu*—the windpipe (trachea)
16. *Sokotsu*—the collar bone
17. *Danchu*—summit of breastbone
18. *Kyototsu*—base of breastbone
19. *Ganchu*—region beneath the nipples
20. *Ekika*—armpit
21. *Kyoei*—area below the armpit
22. *Shinzo*—the heart
23. *Mizouchi*—solar plexus
24. *Denko*—spot between seventh and eighth ribs
25. *Inazuma*—side of body just above hips (floating rib area)
26. *Hozobu*—the navel
27. *Myojo Tanden*—spot approximately one inch below the navel
28. *Uchijakuzawa*—inner part of forearm (where pulse can be felt)
29. *Kinteki*—the testicles
30. *Yako*—inside of upper thigh
31. *Hiza Kansetsu*—knee joint
32. *Kokotsu*—center of shin
33. *Soto Ashi No Kubi*—outside of ankle joint
34. *Uchi Ashi No Kubi*—inside of ankle joint

35. *Ashi No Omote*—outside area of instep
36. *Ashi No Ko*—instep
37. *Kotobu*—back of head (occipital region)
38. *Dokko*—area behind the ears
39. *Keichu*—nape of neck
40. *Katsusatsu*—spot between fifth and sixth vertebra
41. *Soda*—spot between the shoulder blades
42. *Hiji Kansetsu*—elbow joint
43. *Jinzo*—kidneys
44. *Bitei*—the tailbone (coccyx)
45. *Shuko*—back of the hand
46. *Ushiro Inazume*—spot below the buttocks
47. *Ura Hiza*—crease of knee
48. *Achilles Ken*—Achilles tendon

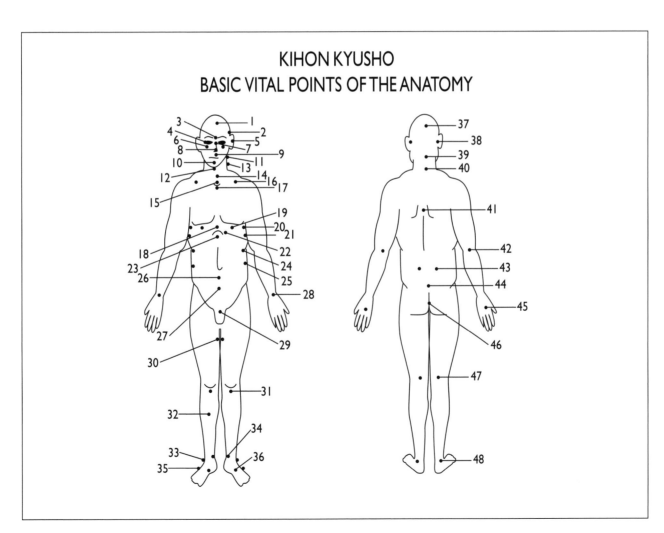

KIHON KYUSHO
BASIC VITAL POINTS OF THE ANATOMY

17

BASIC KINESIOLOGY AS APPLIED TO KARATE TECHNIQUES

Kinesiology may be defined as the study of the mechanics of human motion. An understanding of certain fundamental principles in this area may be helpful in better grasping the rationale behind Karate techniques.

MASS x VELOCITY = FORCE

The faster (velocity) the fist (mass) travels (as in a punch), the greater the impact (force). There are two types of energy: active (kinetic), which is energy in motion, and passive, as in a stretched rubber band or coiled spring. When set into motion these objects become active (kinetic). The further the rubber band is stretched and the tighter the spring is coiled, the more energy they will release. There are two types of muscles: striated muscles (or skeletal muscles) and smooth muscles. Striated muscles are voluntary and react to brain impulses, causing body movements through expansion and contraction. Smooth muscles (such as the muscles in the intestines) lock in and maintain the same tension and force. These muscles use energy more efficiently than striated muscles but are too slow to perform basic, necessary tasks. Striated muscles, on the other hand, are controllable, fast, and easily trained but are less efficient in sustaining activity.

Torque is the motion that creates rotation and moves the torso, thus generating force. Techniques are executed in three stages: the driving stage, the velocity stage, and the impact stage. In the driving stage the body moves toward the target. In the velocity stage the body gains momentum toward the target. The impact stage takes place at the moment when contact is made with the target. There are two types of impact: thrust and snap. Thrust techniques are those that are locked in or pushed through. Snapped techniques are those that are pulled back immediately at contact with the target.

The basic rules of Kinesiology as applied to Karate techniques are as follows:

Rotate the hips to generate torque.

Tense the stomach muscles to create vibration.

Stabilize the position to absorb the shock of impact.

When combined, these principles form the concept of focus *(Kime)* on a physical level.

OUTLINE OF PHYSICAL TECHNIQUES

NATURAL WEAPONS

Te—Hand / *Kaishu* (open hand)

1. *Tegatana* (or *Shuto*)—Hand sword (using *Seiryuto* (ox-jaw)—lower area of hand blade near wrist)
2. *Haito*,Ridge hand
3. *Nukite*—Spear hand
4. *Oya Yubi*—Thumb
5. *Oya Yubi Kansetsu*—Thumb joint
6. *Haishu*—Back of hand
7. *Hirate*—Inside of open hand
8. *Toho*—Y of hand
9. *Tenohida*—Palm heel
10. *Washite*—Eagle hand
11. *Ippon Yubi Saki*—One (index) fingertip
12. *Nihon* (or *Nidan*) *Yubi Saki*—Two fingertips
13. *Kumanote*—Bear hand

Ken (or *Kobushi*)—Fist
1. *Seiken*—Normal fist (using *Kensaki*—first two knuckles)
2. *Uraken*—Back (or reverse side) fist
3. *Kentsui*—Hammer fist
4. *Hanken* (or *Dai Ni Kansetsu*)—Half fist
5. *Ippon Dai Ni Kansetsu*—Second knuckle joint of first finger
6. *Nihon Dai Ni Kansetsu*—Second knuckle joint of second finger

Ude—Arm
1. *Kote* (or *Zenwan*)—Forearm
2. *Hiji*—Elbow

Ashi—Foot and Leg
1. *Tsumasaki*—Spear foot
2. *Josokutei* (or *Haisoku*)—Ball of foot
3. *Ashi No Ko*—Instep
4. *Ashigatana* (or *Sokuto*)—Foot sword (or blade)
5. *Kakato*—Heel
6. *Hiza*—Knee
7. *Mokuzune*—Shin

Atama—Head
1. *Hitai*—Forehead
2. *Ryokado*—Back side of head

A. FOUNDATIONAL TECHNIQUES

TACHI KATA ➝ Stances

(Methods of Planting the Feet)

It should be noted that stances may be classified as: Regimental—stances used for regimentation, as in the case of *Musubi Dachi, Heisoku Dachi, Soto Hachiji Dachi,* etc.; Classical—stances passed down in traditional *Kata,* such as *Tsuru Ashi Dachi, Neko Ashi Dachi, Gyaku Dachi,* etc.; Practical—stances that are functional in combat, such as *Mae Kaga Mi Dachi, Shiko Dachi,* etc. Some stances may fall into more than one category.

Musubi Dachi—Knotted or linked stance (heel to heel)

Heisoku Dachi—Blocked stance (feet together—inside edges touching).

Hachiji Dachi—eight (or figure eight) stance.

Soto Hachiji Dachi—Outside eight stance.

Uchi Hachiji Dachi—Inside eight stance.

Naihanchin Dachi—Horse riding stance.

Sanchin Dachi—Three battle stance (or hourglass stance).

Shiko Dachi—Side or side-straddle stance (four-sided stance).

Mae Kagami Dachi—Forward (bent leg) stance (or *Hanmi*—half-facing posture).

Mae Dachi—Variation of *Mae Kaga Mi Dachi.*

Neko Ashi Dachi—Cat (leg or foot) stance.

Kosa Dachi—Intersecting (or crossed) stance.

Tsuru Ashi (or *Ippon Ashi*) *Dachi*—Crane (or one leg) stance.

Gyaku Dachi (Ushiro Kagami)—Reverse stance.

Kyuho (or *Zenkutsu*) *Dachi*—Forward stance (shoulders squared to the front).

Heiko Dachi—Parallel stance (variation of *Hachji Dachi*).

Soe Dachi—Reinforced stance.

Fuse Dachi—Defensive stance (used in Kushanku Kata only).

(Also other variations)

KAMAE

Guard Positions

Tsuki No Kamae—Punching guard

Sanchin No Kamae—Three battle guard

Shizentai No Kamae—Natural guard

Yoi No Kamae—Ready guard

Seiken No Kamae—Normal fist guard

Tegatana (or *Shuto*) *No Kamae*—Hand sword guard

Kihon No Kamae—Basic guard

Jiyu No Kamae—Free-style guard

Uraken No Kamae—Inverted fist guard

Furiage No Kamae—Front and high guard

Hiraki No Kamae—Front and side guard

Nidan No Kamae—Upper and lower guard

(Also other variations)

TENSHIN WAZA

Body Transfer (Dodging) Technique

Tsuri Ashi (or *Suriashi*)—Slide step

Fumi Dashi—Step or lunge

Oshifumikomi—Slide step lunge or push step

Kosa Su Su Mi—Intersecting (or cross) step

(Koshi) Hineri—(Hip) twist

Furi Muki—Body turn

Yoko Ido—Side move (or step)

    Dai Ichi—No. 1

    Dai Ni—No. 2

    Dai San—No. 3

    Dai Yon—No. 4

Erekae—Leg change

Mawari Komi—Circle step

Mawari Komi Erekae—Circle step leg change

Taore and Ten—Falling and rolling

    Zen Ten (or *Zenpo Kaiten*)—Forward roll

    Ko Ten—Backward roll

    Yoko Ten—Side roll

    Zen Taore—Forward fall

    Ko Taore—Backward fall

    Yoko Taore—Side fall

    Mawashi Taore (or *Tomoe Taore*)—Roundhouse or pinwheel fall

Tobi Komi—Jump step

Tobi Agari—Jump

Kaga Mi—Duck

Bu Bu—Bobbing and weaving

    Yoko Furimi—Side leaning

    Sorimi—Backward leaning

    Hikimi—Pull in

    Ryusui Kaga Mi—Circular ducking

    Others

Sanchin Hoko—Method of stepping or walking used in Sanchin Kata (Crescent or half circle steps)

KOKYU WAZA

Breathing Technique

Shin Kokyu—Relaxed (deep) breathing

Shinsen Kokyu—(rapid) Replenishing breathing

Tsuyoku Haku Kokyu—Forced or tensed breathing

Fukushiki Kokyu—Abdominal breathing

B. PRIMARY TECHNIQUES

UKE WAZA—Blocking Technique

Jodan Age Uke—Upper rising block

Gedan Barai Uke—Lower sweeping block

Uchi Uke—Inside block

Soto Uke—Outside block

Tegatana (or *Shuto*) *Uke*—Hand sword block

Kosa Uke—Intersecting block

Kote Uke—Forearm block

Ashi Uke—Leg block

Nami Gaeshi Uke—Wave change block

Tenohida Uke—Palm heel block

Tekubi Uke—Wrist block

Ura Uke—Inverted (or curved) wrist block

Nagashi Uke—Parry block

Sukui Uke—Scooping block

Haraite Uke—Sweeping block

Hiji Uke—Elbow block

Hasami Uke—Scissor block

Kakete Uke—Hook hand block

Soe Uke—Reinforced block

Nidan Uke—Two-level (or double) block

Mawashi Uke—Roundhouse block

Kakiwake Uke—Wedge block

Osae Uke—Pressing block

Seiken Uke—Normal fist (or punching) block

Morote Uke—Double block

Keito Uke—Chicken head block

TSUKI (OR ZUKI) WAZA

Punching Technique

Maete Tsuki—Front hand or jab

Hineri Tsuki—Twist punch

Tate Tsuki—Vertical punch

Gyaku Tsuki—Reverse punch

Fumidashi Tsuki—Lunge punch

Choku Tsuki—Straight punch

Kagi Tsuki—Hook punch

Ura Tsuki—Inverted (or reverse side) punch

Age Ura Tsuki—Rising inverted (or uppercut) punch

Morote Tsuki—Double punch

Yama Tsuki—Mountian punch

Nidan Tsuki—Bilevel punch

(Also other variations)

NOTE: In defining kicking techniques the terms *Keage* and *Kekomi* are often used. Ke may be defined as "kick" or "kicking." Age may be defined as "rising." When combined, *Keage*. A rising kick is often erroneously considered a snap kick. The correct term is *Kebanashi* or *Keribanashi* (returning kick). *Kekomi* (or *Kerikomi*) may be defined as "kick-in" or "kick-through" a thrust kick whereby the kick goes through the target, as opposed to hitting the target and retracting immediately on contact.

KERI WAZA

Kicking Techniques

Mae Geri—Front kick

Yoko Geri—Side kick

Mawashi Geri—Roundhouse kick

Ushiro Geri—Back kick

Hiza Geri—Knee kick

Fumikomi Geri—Stomping kick

Mawashi Ushiro (or *Ushiro Maru*) *Geri*—Roundhouse back kick

Kaiten Geri—Wheel kick

Kagi Geri—Hook kick

Mae Tobi Geri—Front jump kick

Hiza Tobi Geri—Jump knee kick

Yoko Tobi Geri—Jump side kick

Nidan Tobi Geri—Two-level (or double) front jump kick

Mae Taore Geri—Front fall (or drop) kick

Yoko Taore Geri—Side fall (or drop) kick

Mawashi Taore Geri—Roundhouse fall (or drop) kick

Ushiro Taore Geri—Back fall (or drop) kick

Mikkatsuki Geri—Crescent (or three day moon) kick

Other Kicking Variations

Note: The following kicking techniques are not used for grading and are listed for reference purposes only.

Kakato Geri—Heel kick

Mawashi Tobi Geri—Jump roundhouse kick

Ushiro Tobi Geri—Jump back kick

Mawashi Ushiro Tobi Geri—Jump roundhouse back kick

Kagi Tobi Geri—Jump hook kick

Kaiten Tobi Geri—Jump wheel kick

Kakato Geri Otoshi—Dropping Heel Kick

Gyaku Mikkatsuki Geri—Reverse crescent kick (using blade of the foot)

Gyaku Mikkatsuki Tobi Geri—Jump reverse crescent kick (using blade of the foot)

Hiza Ate Otoshi—Dropping knee smash

Atogata Kakato Geri—Lifting heel kick to the rear

UCHI (OR ATE) WAZA

Striking Technique

Tegatana (or *Shuto) Uchi*—Hand sword (or knife-hand) strike

Haito Uchi—Ridge hand strike

Nukite Uchi—Spear hand strike

Tenohida Uchi—Palm heel strike

Kumanote (Uchi)—Bear hand (strike)

Dai Ni Kansetsu Uchi (or *Hanken*)—Half fist (or second knuckle joint) strike

Ippon Kai Ni Kansetsu Uchi—second knuckle joint of index finger strike

Nihon Dai Ni Kansetsu Uchi—second knuckle joint of middle finger strike

Furi Uchi—Swinging strike

Hiji Ate—Elbow smash

Toho Uchi—"Y" of the hand strike

Washite Uchi—Eagle hand strike

Atama Ate—head smash (or butt)

   Hitai Ate—Forehead smash

   Ryokado Ate—Backside head smash

Uraken Uchi—Inverted (or back) fist strike

Oya Yubi Uchi—Thumb strike

Ippon Yubi Saki Uchi—One-fingertip strike

Nihon Yubi Saki Uchi—Two-fingertip strike

Kote Uchi—Forearm strike

Kentsui Uchi—Hammer fist strike

Haishu Uchi—Back of hand strike

Hirate Uchi—Open-hand strike

Oya Yubi Kansetsu Uchi—Thumb joint strike

C. SECONDARY TECHNIQUES

NAGE NO KATA

Methods of Throwing

Hiki Otoshi Nage—Pull-down throw

Kubi Nage—Neck throw

Seoinage—Shoulder throw

Shiho Nage—Four-corner throw

Koshi Nage—Hip throw

Kane Basami—Crab scissors

Ashi Barai—Foot (or leg) sweep

Tomoenage—Somersault (or stomach) throw

Hiki Ashi Nage—Pulling leg throw

Hiza Hineri—Knee twist

Ashi Sukui Nage—Leg scoop throw

Sudori Nage—Momentum throw

Ashi Hasami—Leg scissors

Tani Otoshi—Valley drop

Soto Nage—Outside throw

Uchi Nage—Inside throw

Kaiten Ashi Barai—Wheel foot (or leg) sweep

Tenkan Nage—Turning (or reversal) throw

Tsubamegaeshi Nage—Swallow change throw

Morote Gari—Two-hand reaping (or pick up) throw

Irimi Nage—Entering throw

Ura Hiza Fumikomi—Knee crease stomp

Kaiten Nage—Wheel throw

Ushiro Nage—Rear throw

Sutemi Nage—Sacrifice throw

(Also other variations)

SHIME WAZA

Choking Technique

Hadaka Jime (Zen and *Ko)*—Naked choke (front and back)

Kataha Jime—One side choke

Okuri Eri Jime (Zen and *Ko)*—Sliding lapel choke (front and back)

Namijuji Jime (Zen and *Ko)*—Natural cross choke (front and back)

Gyakujuji Jime (Zen and *Ko)*—Reverse cross choke (front and back)

Katajuji Jime (Zen and *Ko)*—Half cross choke (front and back)

Tsukami Jime—Fingertip choke

Tsukikomi Jime—Poking choke

Sode Guruma Jime—Lapel wheel choke

Kesa Gatame Jime—Cross-chest choke

Sankaku Jime—Triangle choke

(Also other variations)

GYAKU-TE
(or GYAKU KANSETSU) WAZA

Reverse Hand (or Joint Reversal) Techniques

Ganseki Otoshi—Boulder drop

Juji Gatame—Cross arm lock

Ude Kujiki—Arm bar

Kote Gaeshi—Outward wrist twist

Hiji Garami—Elbow entanglement

Ude Hishigi—Armlock

Ude Garami—Entangled armlock

Kote Hineri—Forearm twist

Oshi Taoshi—Push down

Hiki Taoshi—Pull down

Ude Hineri—Arm twist

Ude Gaeshi—Arm turn

Jun Tedori—Regular twist

Gyaku Tedori—Reverse twist

Ikajo—First control

Nikajo—Second control

Sankajo—Third control

ASHI KANSETSU WAZA

Leg / Foot Joint Techniques

Ashi Hishigi—Leg / foot lock

Ashi Garami—Leg / foot entanglement

Ashi Hineri—Leg / foot twist

Ashi Kudaki—Leg / foot crushing

(Also other variations)

HAZUSHI WAZA

Seizure-escaping Techniques

(Many Variations)

GOSHINJUTSU

Self-defense Art

A term use to describe various techniques of self-defense.

GENERAL TECHNIQUES

1. *Tori Waza*—Holding (or grabbing) techniques
   Ashi Tori—Leg holding
   Kakete—Hook hand (also *Dakite*—hugging hand)
   Hikite—Pull hand
   Tsukami—Fingertip grab
   Kumanote—Bear hand grab
   (Also other variations)
2. *Kyo* (or *Kyo Waza*)—Faking and feinting techniques
3. *Renzoku* (or *Renraku*) *Waza*—Combination (or continuous) techniques
4. *Katame Waza*—Grappling techniques
5. *Suwari Waza*—Seated techniques
6. *Osae Waza*—Pinning or holding down techniques
7. *Shirahaderi*—Defense against bladed weapons
   A. *Tanto Dori*—Knife taking (or knife defense)
   B. *Tachi Dori*—Sword taking (or sword defense)
8. *Ne Waza*—Ground techniques
9. *Kenju Bogyo*—Gun defense
(Also other variations)

KIHON WAZA

Basic Technique

The photos included in this section are examples of basic techniques taken from the foundational, primary, and secondary categories. It should be noted that there are a variety of methods that may be used in executing techniques (e.g. from a stable position, with movement, using the front or rear arm, the front or rear leg, etc.).

The techniques illustrated here are a random sampling chosen to convey a fundamental and practical application.

UKE WAZA ➤ Blocking Techniques

ASHI UKE
Leg Block

GEDAN BARAI UKE
Low Sweeping Block

HIJI UKE
Elbow Block

NAGASHI UKE
Parry Block

TSUKI (ZUKI) WAZA ➤ Punching Techniques

TATE TSUKI (MAETE)
Vertical Punch (Front Hand)—Jab

KAGI TSUKI (MAETE)
Hook Punch (Front Hand)

GYAKU TSUKI (HINERI)
Reverse Punch (Twisting)

AGE URA TSUKI
(Uppercut)

KERI WAZA ← Kicking Techniques

MAE GERI—Front Kick

YOKO GERI—Side Kick

HIZA GERI—Knee Kick

MAWASHI GERI—Roundhouse Kick

USHIRO GERI—Back Kick

UCHI (ATE) WAZA ➤ Striking Techniques

URAKEN UCHI—Backfist Strike

TEGATANA (OR SHUTO) UCHI—Handsword Strike

TENOHIDA UCHI—Palm Heel Strike

HIJE ATE—Elbow Strike

OSHI HIZA NAGE ➤ Pushing Knee Throw

MOROTE GARI NAGE ◆ Double Reap Throw

HADAKA JIME (USHIRO A.K.A. KO) ◆ Naked Strangle—Rear

HADAKA JIME (MAE A.K.A. ZEN) ➤ Naked Strangle—Front

SOTO GYAKU TEKUBI HINERI ➤ Outside Reverse Wrist Twist

MAE SHIME (JIME) HAZUSHI ➤ Escape from Front Choke

USHIRO KUMADAKE HAZUSHI ◆ Rear Bear Hug Escape

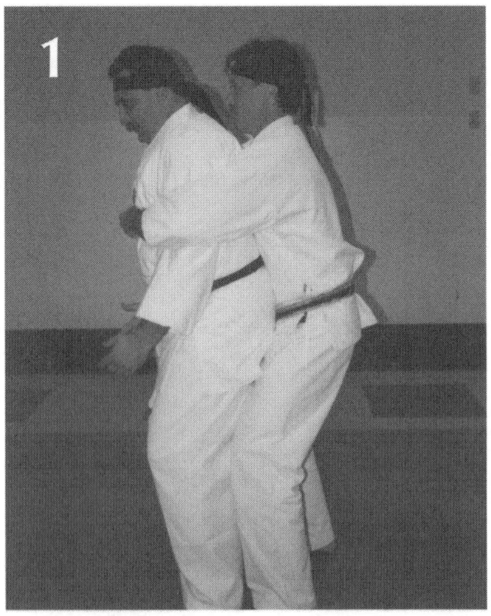

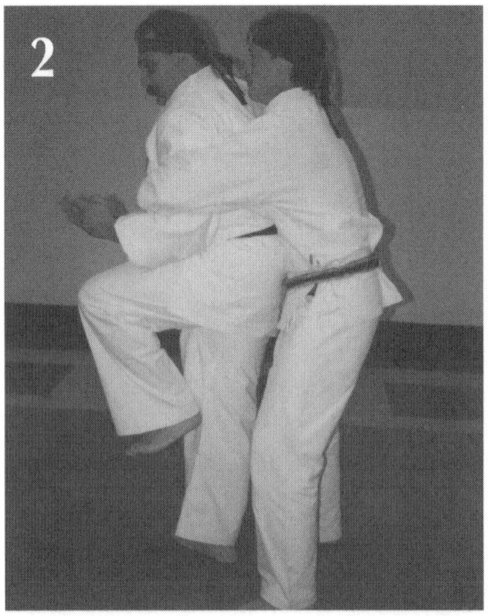

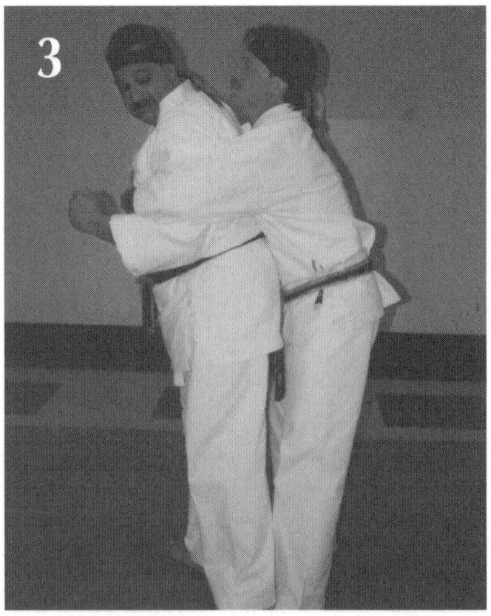

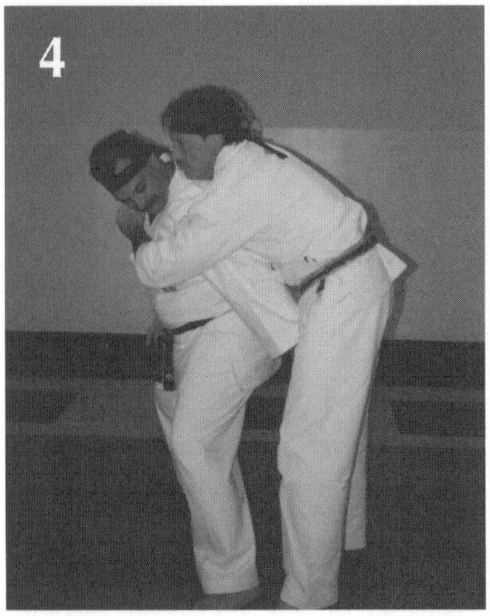

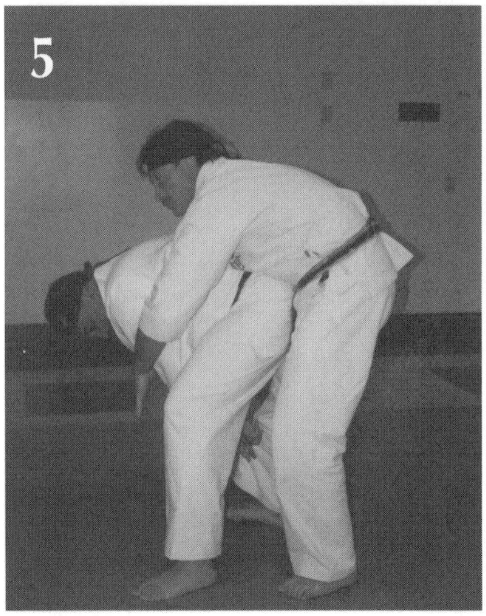

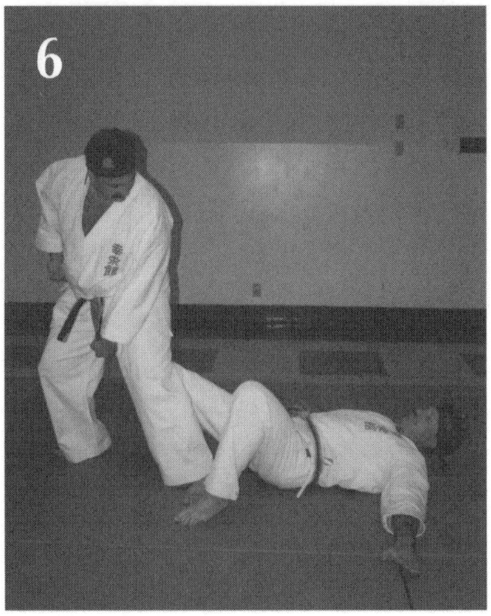

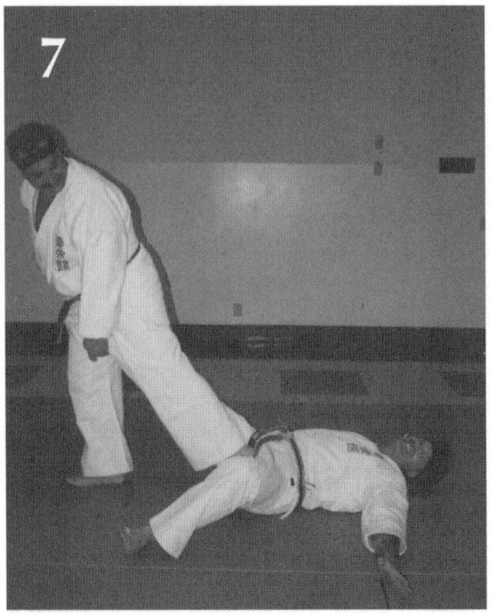

AUTHOR'S CONCLUSION

As earlier stated in this text, there are many paths to the mountain. If we reach the peak, we will all view the same moon; however, the wrong path leads nowhere. The journey to self improvement/enlightenment is often a lonely one. Perhaps the greatest lesson my teacher transmitted to me was the principle of how to think, as opposed to what to think.

Each of us must choose an order of moral priorities. It is the goal of the Budo (Martial Way) to aid us in finding a just, constructive, happy, healthy, prosperous middle course in life which will enhance our overall existence. This pursuit is never ending. All things in life change, with the exception of human nature. Be guided by wisdom and never led by ignorance.

ABOUT THE AUTHOR

Brian Frost is the holder of a 7th degree black belt (Nanadan/Shichidan) and an International Instructor's Certificate (Kokusai Shihan Menkyo) in Karate. He is a direct pupil of Master Onishi Eizo, founder of the Koei-Kan system of Karate-Do and Chairman of the All-Japan Karate-Do Association.

Mr. Frost served his apprenticeship under Master Onishi and studied in Japan as an Uchi Deshi (live-in disciple) at the Master's home.

As one of Master Onishi's senior students, Mr. Frost serves as the Chief Technical Instructor and National Director for Koei-Kan in the United States. In 1972 Mr. Frost captured the All-Japan Koei-Kan Championship held in the Kamata Sports Stadium in Tokyo and has competed, instructed and demonstrated world-wide. Mr. Frost became acquainted with western style boxing at an early age (eventually accruing an amateur record of 21–3) and began the study of Karate during the early 1960's. With more than thirty years of experience in Karate, Mr. Frost continues to be a guiding force in the promulgation of the Koei-Kan system. He is currently based in the Detroit - Metropolitan area.